ROUTINE ABUSE, ROUTINE DENIAL

Civil Rights and the Political Crisis in Bahrain

Human Rights Watch/Middle East

Human Rights Watch
New York · Washington · London · Brussels

485 Fifth Avenue, New York, NY 10017-6104
Tel: (212) 972-8400, Fax: (212) 972-0905, E-mail: hrwnyc@hrw.org

1522 K Street, N.W., #910, Washington, DC 20005-1202
Tel: (202) 371-6592, Fax: (202) 371-0124, E-mail: hrwdc@hrw.org

33 Islington High Street, N1 9LH London, UK
Tel: (171) 713-1995, Fax: (171) 713-1800, E-mail: hrwatchuk@gn.apc.org

15 Rue Van Campenhout, 1000 Brussels, Belgium
Tel: (2) 732-2009, Fax: (2) 732-0471, E-mail: hrwatcheu@gn.apc.org

Web Site Address: http://www.hrw.org
Gopher Address://gopher.humanrights.org:5000/11/int/hrw
Listserv address: To subscribe to the list, send an e-mail message to
majordomo@igc.apc.org with "subscribe hrw-news" in the body of the message
(leave the subject line blank).

Human Rights Watch is dedicated to
protecting the human rights of people around the world.

We stand with victims and activists to prevent
discrimination, to uphold political freedom, to protect people from
inhumane conduct in wartime, and to bring offenders to justice.

We investigate and expose
human rights violations and hold abusers accountable.

We challenge governments and those who hold power to end
abusive practices and respect international human rights law.

We enlist the public and the international
community to support the cause of human rights for all.

HUMAN RIGHTS WATCH

Human Rights Watch conducts regular, systematic investigations of human rights abuses in some seventy countries around the world. Our reputation for timely, reliable disclosures has made us an essential source of information for those concerned with human rights. We address the human rights practices of governments of all political stripes, of all geopolitical alignments, and of all ethnic and religious persuasions. Human Rights Watch defends freedom of thought and expression, due process and equal protection of the law, and a vigorous civil society; we document and denounce murders, disappearances, torture, arbitrary imprisonment, discrimination, and other abuses of internationally recognized human rights. Our goal is to hold governments accountable if they transgress the rights of their people.

Human Rights Watch began in 1978 with the founding of its Helsinki division. Today, it includes five divisions covering Africa, the Americas, Asia, the Middle East, as well as the signatories of the Helsinki accords. It also includes three collaborative projects on arms transfers, children's rights, and women's rights. It maintains offices in New York, Washington, Los Angeles, London, Brussels, Moscow, Dushanbe, Rio de Janeiro, and Hong Kong. Human Rights Watch is an independent, nongovernmental organization, supported by contributions from private individuals and foundations worldwide. It accepts no government funds, directly or indirectly.

The staff includes Kenneth Roth, executive director; Michele Alexander, development director; Cynthia Brown, program director; Barbara Guglielmo, finance and administration director; Robert Kimzey, publications director; Jeri Laber, special advisor; Lotte Leicht, Brussels office director; Susan Osnos, communications director; Jemera Rone, counsel; Wilder Tayler, general counsel; and Joanna Weschler, United Nations representative.

The regional directors of Human Rights Watch are Peter Takirambudde, Africa; José Miguel Vivanco, Americas; Sidney Jones, Asia; Holly Cartner, Helsinki; and Eric Goldstein, Middle East (acting). The project directors are Joost R. Hiltermann, Arms Project; Lois Whitman, Children's Rights Project; and Dorothy Q. Thomas, Women's Rights Project.

The members of the board of directors are Robert L. Bernstein, chair; Adrian W. DeWind, vice chair; Roland Algrant, Lisa Anderson, William Carmichael, Dorothy Cullman, Gina Despres, Irene Diamond, Fiona Druckenmiller, Edith Everett, Jonathan Fanton, James C. Goodale, Jack Greenberg, Vartan Gregorian, Alice H. Henkin, Stephen L. Kass, Marina Pinto Kaufman, Bruce Klatsky, Harold Hongju Koh, Alexander MacGregor, Josh Mailman, Samuel K. Murumba, Andrew Nathan, Jane Olson, Peter Osnos, Kathleen Peratis, Bruce Rabb, Sigrid Rausing, Anita Roddick, Orville Schell, Sid Sheinberg, Gary G. Sick, Malcolm Smith, Domna Stanton, Maureen White, and Maya Wiley.

ABOUT THIS REPORT

Material for this report was gathered by Human Rights Watch/Middle East between March 1996 and February 1997. The government of Bahrain rejected our request to send an official information-gathering mission to the country. Human Rights Watch representatives did visit Bahrain briefly nonetheless, where they met with defense lawyers and persons who had been detained by the authorities, as well as prominent persons in various professions and in business. Because of the unauthorized nature of the visit, however, Human Rights Watch was unable to speak with government officials, and our access to persons in neighborhoods under surveillance was severely constricted. In addition, Bahrainis living in the country, even lawyers and prominent businesspeople, agreed to speak with Human Rights Watch only on condition that they not be identified. We also met with Bahrainis living in exile in Dubai, Kuwait, Beirut, Damascus, London, Lund and Copenhagen, and with Bahrainis living in and visiting the United States. Interviews referred to in the text, unless the location of the interview is specified, took place outside of Bahrain.

This report was written by Joe Stork, advocacy director of Human Rights Watch/Middle East. Steve Rothman, intern at Human Rights Watch/Middle East, and Shira Robinson, Human Rights Watch/Middle East associate, provided greatly appreciated research assistance. Clary Bencomo and Gamal Abouali of Human Rights Watch/Middle East helped with the translation of Arabic documents. Kuwaiti human rights activists who cannot be named provided translation assistance with interviews conducted in that country. Several Bahraini lawyers also provided invaluable assistance and clarifications on points of Bahraini law, but they cannot be named for reasons of personal safety. Said Essaloumi, of Article 19, kindly shared with Human Rights Watch an unpublished report covering press freedom issues in Bahrain.

This report was edited by Jeri Laber, senior advisor to Human Rights Watch, and Eric Goldstein, acting executive director of Human Rights Watch/Middle East. Shira Robinson and Awali Samara, Human Rights Watch/Middle East associates, prepared the text for publication.

CONTENTS

1. INTRODUCTION

Human rights abuses in Bahrain are wide-ranging and fall into two basic categories. The first relates to law enforcement and administration of justice issues. These encompass the behavior of security forces toward those under arrest and detention, and when confronting civil disturbances; arbitrary detention; physical and psychological abuse of detainees; denial of access to legal counsel; and denial of the right to a swift and impartial judicial hearing. The second area of human rights violations relates to the broad denial of fundamental political rights and civil liberties, including freedom of expression, freedom of association and assembly, and the right to participate in the conduct of public affairs. In terms of numbers of people affected, the situation has been particularly acute since the end of 1994, with the onset of a period of protracted civil unrest that has continued into the spring of 1997.[1] This unrest has increasingly taken on the coloration of a sectarian conflict between the majority Shi`a population and the Sunni ruling family and military-political establishment. The government of Bahrain has dismissed the unrest as the work of "Hizb Allah terrorists" instigated and supported by Iran.

Respect for human rights has long been problematic in Bahrain, and many abusive practices derive from the policies pursued by Great Britain prior to independence in 1971. From the early 20th century on, British colonial rule grafted numerous legal and administrative reforms onto a tribal form of local political authority centered around the Al Khalifa family. These reforms were also propelled by the transition from an economy organized mainly around feudal-type estates to a more complex commercial and industrial economy based on oil production and export. In the pre-independence period, as rule of law was constructed in numerous domains, political challenges to local and colonial authority continued to be dealt with in summary fashion, with little regard to emerging international norms of political and civil rights.

The first years of independence, from 1972 to 1975, constituted an interlude of sorts. A partially-elected constituent assembly constructed a constitution that endorsed a wide range of internationally recognized civil and political rights and called for a National Assembly of thirty elected and up to

---

[1] As of mid-May, at least twenty-nine deaths have been attributed to the unrest: fifteen were of Bahraini citizens who were killed by security forces, including several who died in police custody; three were of security personnel; one person was killed by an explosive device, allegedly while detonating the device at a bank in June 1996; and ten expatriate workers were killed in arson attacks.

1

fourteen appointed cabinet ministers *ex officio,* with powers to review (though not initiate) legislation and interrogate members of the government. Although political parties remained illegal, a national campaign and elections in 1973 led to the emergence of three relatively distinct groupings—a so-called People's Bloc, mainly leftists and Arab nationalists; a Religious Bloc comprising teachers and religious court judges mainly from rural constituencies; and an Independent Middle.

The political detente between the ruling Al Khalifa family and the disparate forces of civil society came apart in 1975, when the government was unable to obtain National Assembly approval of a State Security Measures Law, which authorized arrest and imprisonment for up to three years without charge or trial for undefined "acts" or "statements" that could be construed to threaten the country's internal or external security. In August 1975, the government dissolved the National Assembly by decree. The constitution stipulates that in such an event elections for a new assembly must be held within two months. This the ruling family, nearly twenty-two years later, has steadfastly refused to do, and this refusal is one major factor underlying the current unrest.

In 1976, the year following the dissolution of the assembly, the government decreed a new penal code that substantively nullified many of the civil liberties and political rights protected by the constitution and effectively criminalized a wide range of nonviolent political activities. Over the more than two decades of unconstitutional rule by decree that have followed, other decrees discussed in this report have further undermined basic political and due process rights. As a consequence, Bahrain since 1975 is country where citizens risk search and seizure, and incarceration without charge or trial, for speaking out publicly in a manner that the government regards as hostile or critical. Public advocacy of restoring the National Assembly provisions of the constitution falls into this category. Communications among citizens, and between residents and persons outside Bahrain, are monitored. Political parties and organizations are proscribed, as are independent trade unions. Public meetings and gatherings require prior authorization, which in practice is not given. Radio and television media is directly controlled by the state; a combination of state censorship and stringent self-censorship rules out critical discussion in print of domestic politics or of relations with neighboring states. Abuses that are categorically forbidden by Bahrain's constitution, as well as by international law, such as torture and forced exile, are practiced routinely, as matters of state policy.

Recent decrees have expanded the articles of the penal code coming under the jurisdiction of the so-called State Security Court, where most due process protections are absent. Among the thousands of persons detained in the course of the past two-and-a-half years of protracted unrest, most who have been charged have been tried before the security court. Defendants wait many months, sometimes more than a year, to be tried. According to defense lawyers and former detainees, beatings and other forms physical and psychological abuse in the course of arrest and during detention are common and are frequently administered by security personnel as a form of extra-judicial punishment. This abuse becomes especially severe when used to secure confessions, and frequently amounts to torture. A person brought before the security court first meets his or her lawyer only on the day of the first hearing, and subsequent meetings in practice occur only at the time of subsequent court hearings. Security court sessions are generally held *in camera*. Uncorroborated confessions, secured in the absence of counsel, are sufficient for conviction. Judgments of the security court cannot be appealed. There are no instances known to Human Rights Watch where Bahraini authorities have conducted an investigation as a result of allegations of torture, or where anyone in a position of responsibility has been disciplined for committing such acts.

The government of Bahrain denies that it sanctions torture or other forms of physical abuse in any manner. The government also maintains that its policies do not in any way violate international human rights standards. In response to a letter to the government from Human Rights Watch, Bahrain's ambassador in Washington, Dr. Muhammad Abdul Ghaffar, wrote, "The allegations made against Bahrain originate from a very small, but skillful group of fundamentalist zealots and extremists, who are connected to terrorists in Bahrain.... They have disseminated their propaganda through manipulation of the media and of the international human rights movement."[2] At the same time, the government's repeated refusal to grant visas to allow independent human rights monitors to conduct research or attend trials undermines the credibility of such denials. Bahrain is not a state party to the International Covenant on Civil and Political Rights (ICCPR) or to the Convention against Torture and Other Cruel, Inhuman or Degrading Treatment or Punishment (CAT).[3] The government recently reached an agreement with the International Committee of the Red Cross (ICRC) to inspect prisons and interview detainees, and the ICRC began conducting visits in November 1996. While this is a positive development, it is no guarantee that abuses

---

[2] The text of the Human Rights Watch letter and the ambassador's response appear as appendices to this report.

[3] Of the major international rights covenants, Bahrain is a state party to the International Convention on the Elimination of All Forms of Racial Discrimination and the Convention on the Rights of the Child.

will be exposed because the ICRC as a matter of policy keeps its findings confidential and shares them only with the government of Bahrain.

The government of Bahrain's dismissal of the country's political unrest as Iranian-sponsored "terrorism" has enjoyed the public support of Arab states in the region, especially Saudi Arabia. Bahrain's most important military and political allies outside the region are the United States and the United Kingdom. Bahrain is the site of the headquarters of the U.S. Navy's Fifth Fleet, and the country has generally supported U.S. military and strategic policy in the Persian Gulf. The U.S. is the Bahrain Defense Force's major source of weapons. Washington has publicly endorsed Bahrain's attribution of responsibility for its unrest to Iranian meddling, and, except for the Bahrain chapter in its annual *Country Reports on Human Rights Practices*, has refused to speak out critically about the human rights situation in the country. The U.K.'s approach has been similar to that of the U.S., although, perhaps owing to the presence in London of a vocal Bahraini opposition community, it has publicly expressed concern in very general terms about human rights practices of the government of Bahrain.

2. RECOMMENDATIONS

To the government of Bahrain concerning law enforcement and administration of justice:

- Amend the State Security Measures Law of 1974, the Penal Code of 1976, and all other laws and decrees to eliminate those provisions that violate rights protected by Bahrain's Constitution, including those provisions that allow for unlimited or arbitrary detention. Enact amendments to those laws that will ensure the rights of a detainee to challenge promptly the lawfulness of his or her detention before a judicial authority and to have prompt access to family and legal counsel in accordance with international standards.

- End the practice of detaining persons for unlimited or extended periods without charge or trial for vaguely-defined "acts" or "statements." Release immediately all persons being so detained or bring formal charges and try those persons in a court of law in which they have full access to defense counsel, the right to call defense witnesses and to question prosecution witnesses, and the right to appeal the verdict to a higher judicial tribunal in accordance with international fair trial standards.

- Ensure that members of the Ministry of Interior directorates of Public Security, Criminal Investigations, and State Security comply with the requirements of the criminal procedure code and with international law enforcement standards in conducting arrests and searches of premises.

- Establish by legislation, in accordance with the constitution of the state of Bahrain, a Supreme Council of the Judiciary to supervise the functions of the courts (Article 102[d]) and a judicial body competent to rule on the constitutionality of laws and regulations (Article 103).

- End the practice of interrogating detainees without allowing them to exercise their right to legal counsel. Release or conduct an independent judicial review of the cases of all persons convicted solely on the basis of uncorroborated confessions secured without the presence of defense counsel. This review should take the form of a public hearing involving the accused and legal counsel of his or her choice.

- Abolish the State Security Court and end the practice of trying detainees before any tribunal that is closed to the public and in which basic fair trial

5

standards are not guaranteed. Release all persons convicted by the State Security Court, or conduct an independent judicial review of their cases and reverse or amend convictions and sentences accordingly. This review should take the form of a public hearing involving the accused and legal counsel of his or her choice.

- Transfer the office of public prosecutor from the Ministry of Interior to the Ministry of Justice and Islamic Affairs, and take other steps as necessary to separate institutionally the state's public security and the administration of justice functions.

- Appoint a special independent public prosecutor to investigate deaths at the hands of the security forces, including those occurring in detention, and alleged acts of torture and cruel, inhuman, and degrading treatment committed by officers with the Special Investigation Service, the Criminal Investigation Directorate, and the Public Security Force. This prosecutor should be empowered to report publicly on the findings of such an investigation and to bring charges against any officials implicated as responsible for ordering, for carrying out, or for tolerating such acts of torture or acts resulting in wrongful death. The special prosecutor should receive the firm public backing of the head of state, Amir Isa bin Salman Al Khalifa, and have a length of tenure sufficient to ensure independence.

- Appoint an independent commission to investigate overall law enforcement and administration of justice under the Ministry of Interior and the Ministry of Justice and Islamic Affairs, and to recommend changes in the 1976 Penal Code and in the administration of justice that will bring that administration into compliance with Bahrain's constitution and with international standards.

- Establish a public register of all detainees, in accordance with international standards, that will include names and whereabouts of those arrested, time of arrest, by which order and under what charge, to be updated on a frequent and regular basis and made available without restriction to judges, lawyers, families, and human rights organizations.

- Enact legislation that will allow victims of torture, prolonged or arbitrary detention, and other gross abuses of basic human rights, or their families, to obtain compensation from the government and from those responsible for such violations.

- Take immediate steps to ratify the International Covenant on Civil and Political Rights and the Convention against Torture and Other Cruel and Inhuman or Degrading Treatment or Punishment.

To the government of Bahrain concerning the provision of basic political rights:

- Amend the 1976 Penal Code to eliminate or modify those articles and provisions that unduly restrict the ability of Bahraini citizens to exercise peacefully their rights to freedom of assembly, association, and expression, in particular Articles 134A, 163, 164, 165, 168, 169, 178, and 222.

- Restore the right of Bahraini citizens to participate in public affairs and governance, directly or by means of freely elected representatives, in accordance with international law and with Chapter Two of Bahrain's constitution.

- In accordance with Article 26 of the constitution, end the practice of monitoring postal, telephone, and electronic communications among persons inside Bahrain and with persons outside the country, except when subjected to the oversight of an independent judicial authority.

- End the practice of forcibly exiling Bahraini citizens and announce that Bahrainis living in exile are free to return to the country. If the authorities have reason to believe that a person returning from exile is guilty of a crime, that person may be formally charged and tried before a court of law in which he or she has full access to defense counsel and the right to call defense witnesses and to question prosecution witnesses, and to appeal the verdict to a higher judicial tribunal in accordance with the law.

- Amend the Law of Social and Cultural Societies and Clubs so as to eliminate all unreasonable obstacles to nonviolent political and trade union activity.

•   Amend Amiri Decree No. 14/1979 with Respect to Publications in order to eliminate undue restrictions on the right to freedom of expression and to receive information.

•   Restore civilian leadership to the Ministry of Education and Bahrain University, and restore a policy of faculty recruitment and student admissions to the university that does not discriminate against persons based on their religion or their political opinions.

•   Take steps to regularize the status of Bahrain's *biduun* population—long-term residents without nationality—by facilitating their applications for citizenship and passports and by permitting the return to Bahrain of *biduun* who have been arbitrarily or summarily deported.

•   Allow international and Bahraini human rights workers to exercise their rights to seek, receive, and disseminate information in Bahrain concerning the human rights situation there.

To the United States:
To the Clinton administration:
        The high-level and long-standing political and military relationship between the U.S. and Bahraini governments presents the opportunity for the U.S. to take an overdue vocal and assertive role in addressing recurrent human rights violations in Bahrain. U.S. government officials have told Human Rights Watch that U.S. concerns in this regard are conveyed regularly to the government of Bahrain by the U.S. ambassador in Manama. If this is indeed the case, there are no signs that demarches at this level, and in this fashion, are producing any results. We therefore urge the Clinton administration, as a matter of high priority, to:

•   Publicly criticize human rights abuses by the government of Bahrain that are recurrent, systematic, and matters of state policy, and discontinue the policy of public silence concerning those abuses.

•   Raise the issues discussed in this report with Bahraini officials at the highest levels, and urge the government of Bahrain to take specific and measurable steps toward implementing the above recommendations.

- Instruct the embassy staff in Manama to request permission to attend trials in state security courts and to demonstrate U.S. concern about court proceedings that fall short of international fair-trial standards.

- Instruct Assistant Secretary of State for Democracy, Rights and Labor John Shattuck to focus more of his attention and his office's resources on the human rights problems of the Middle East, including Bahrain.

- Ensure that Bahrain's compliance with international human rights standards is on the agenda of all meetings between high-level U.S. and Bahraini officials, including meetings during visits of U.S. military and Department of Defense officials.

- Instruct the embassy staff in Manama to request the right to visit Shaikh Abd al-Amir al-Jamri, in order to demonstrate U.S. concern about the lengthy detention without charge or trial of persons for whom no evidence has been divulged that they have committed or advocated acts of violence.

- Request the embassy staff in Manama to improve its monitoring and accurate reporting of human rights in Bahrain, as reflected in the Bahrain chapter of the annual U.S. State Department *Country Reports*, by subjecting to greater critical scrutiny the claims of the government with regard to its policies and by assessing directly and without innuendo the accuracy of allegations of government violations made by the Bahrain Human Rights Organization and the Committee for the Defense of Human Rights in Bahrain.

- Make clear to the government of Bahrain, both publicly and privately, that persistent and recurrent human rights violations will affect negatively the depth and quality of relations with the United States, including military and security relations, and that improved respect for human rights will, by contrast, strengthen those relations.

- Instruct the ambassador in Manama and visiting U.S. military and diplomatic officials to raise the issue of human rights in interviews with Bahraini media.

- Urge the government of Bahrain to ratify the International Covenant on Civil and Political Rights and the Convention against Torture.

- Request the government of Bahrain publicly to respond positively to requests by international human rights organizations for visas to conduct research missions.

To Members of Congress:
- Schedule hearings before the House International Relations and the Senate Foreign Relations Committees in which the human rights record of the Bahraini government is explicitly on the agenda.

- Question administration officials, during hearings and briefings on Middle East and Persian Gulf developments, about human rights developments in Bahrain.

- Request the administration to assess and report publicly on steps being taken by the government of Bahrain to ensure basic civil and political rights for all Bahraini citizens.

To the United Kingdom:
The close and long-standing political and military relations between the governments of the United Kingdom and Bahrain give the United Kingdom an important role in bringing about an improvement in Bahrain's human rights record. Officials of the former Conservative Party-led government have told Human Rights Watch and other human rights organizations that they regularly raise these issues with the government of Bahrain on a confidential basis. As discussed above with regard to the U.S., this form of intervention can no longer be regarded as adequate or sufficient. Human Rights Watch therefore urges the government of the United Kingdom, as a matter of priority, to:

- Publicly criticize human rights abuses by the government of Bahrain that are recurrent, systematic, and matters of state policy, and discontinue the policy of public silence concerning those abuses.

- Raise the issues discussed in this report with Bahraini officials at the highest levels and urge the government of Bahrain to take specific and measurable steps toward implementing the above recommendations.

- Instruct the U.K. embassy staff in Manama to request permission to attend trials in security courts and to demonstrate concern about court proceedings that fall short of international fair-trial standards.

- Ensure that Bahrain's compliance with international human rights standards is on the agenda of all meetings between high-level U.K. and Bahraini officials, including meetings during visits of Ministry of Defense as well as Foreign and Commonwealth Office officials to Bahrain.

- Instruct the U.K. embassy staff in Manama to request the right to visit Shaikh Abd al-Amir al-Jamri, in order to demonstrate concern about the lengthy detention without charge or trial of persons for whom no evidence has been divulged that they have committed or advocated acts of violence.

- Make clear to the government of Bahrain, both publicly and privately, that persistent and recurrent human rights violations will affect negatively the depth and quality of relations with the United Kingdom, including military and security relations, and that improved respect for human rights will, by contrast, strengthen those relations.

- Urge the government of Bahrain to ratify the International Covenant on Civil and Political Rights and the Convention against Torture.

- Request the government of Bahrain publicly to respond positively to requests by international human rights organizations for visas to conduct research missions.

3. HISTORICAL BACKGROUND

Bahrain takes its name, which means "two seas" in Arabic, from the main island of a small archipelago located in the Persian Gulf about midway along the Arabian littoral and some 25 kilometers by causeway from Dhahran, Saudi Arabia. The country's total area is 694 kilometers, about four times that of the District of Columbia. The main island (89 percent of this total area), along with the smaller islands of Muharraq and Sitra, account for virtually all of the population and economic activity.[4]

The population in 1996 was around 598,000, of which some 62 percent are Bahraini nationals and the rest workers from South Asia and other Arab countries.[5] Eighty-five percent of the people live in the country's two cities, Manama and al-Muharraq, or in main towns such as Jidd Hafs, Sitra, al-Rifaa or Madinat Isa in the northern third of the country, making Bahrain one of the most highly urbanized countries in the world. Manama's expansion over the past thirty-five years has transformed many of the surrounding villages and towns into suburbs of the capital. A similar process has fused the villages of Sitra into one large town.

Bahrain has historically been a center for regional trade, and Bahrain's local population comprises several distinct elements. About 70 percent are Shi`a Muslims; most of these are the original Arab people of the islands, known as Baharna. There is also a small community descendant from Iranian Shi`a migrants.

---

[4] Eric Hooglund, "Bahrain," in Helen C. Metz, ed., *Persian Gulf States: Country Studies* (Washington, D.C.: U.S. Government Printing Office, 1994), pp. 114, 117. The islet of Umm al-Nasan, off the western coast, is the private property of the ruler, Amir Isa bin Salman Al Khalifa, and the site of his game preserve. The islet of Jiddah, formerly the site of a state prison, is presently the private property of Prime Minister Khalifa bin Salman Al Khalifa, who is also the amir's brother.

[5] Figures provided by the Central Census Directorate, Manama. There are also some 10,000 Bahraini *biduun*—persons without nationality. Many of these have been resident in Bahrain for several generations or more. Most are Shi`a of Persian origin, but a minority are Sunni Arabs.

The number of *biduun* is from the U.S. State Department *Country Report 1996* chapter on Bahrain. For a study of human rights issues involving the larger *biduun* population in Kuwait, see Human Rights Watch/Middle East, *The Bedoons of Kuwait* (New York: Human Rights Watch, 1995).

The Sunnis, approximately 30 percent of the total, include the descendants of the tribes that accompanied the Al Khalifa family conquest of the island in 1783, after nearly two centuries of Persian rule. The other components of the Sunni population are the descendants of Arabs who migrated from the Najd region of north central Arabia, also in the late 18th century, and Arabs, Iranians, Indians, and others who migrated (or in some cases returned) to Bahrain and eastern Arabia.[6] These communal distinctions, and especially the relative Sunni monopolization of political power and land ownership under the ruling Al Khalifa family, have played a key role in the island's political dynamics to this day.[7]

Bahrain's 20th century political and socioeconomic history is dominated by two factors. The first is British rule: from 1868 until the country's formal independence in 1971, Bahrain was essentially a British protectorate. The primacy of the Al Khalifa family is one consequence, and hereditary rule by the Al Khalifa amir (prince) is now enshrined in Article 1 of the 1973 Constitution. The present amir, Isa bin Salman Al Khalifa, was born in 1933 and became amir in 1961. A British Political Agent resided in Manama beginning around the turn of the century and played an increasing role in local affairs. After World War II, Britain's

---

[6] Rosemarie Said Zahlan, *The Making of the Modern Gulf States* (London: Unwin Hyman, 1989), pp. 46-48.

[7] Fuad Khuri (*Tribe and State in Bahrain,* University of Chicago Press, 1980) observes that by the late 19th century, as Al Khalifa rule was consolidated under Isa bin Ali, the islands came to resemble a "feudal estate system" in which increasing amounts of cultivated land—which altogether was not more than five percent of Bahrain's total land area—came under the direct "administration" of the Al Khalifa. With the British-sponsored administrative reforms of the 1920s, these administered fiefs were converted into private ownership (pp. 35, 41). Land titles were also allocated to leaders of allied Sunni tribes, enabling them "to make a comfortable living as rentiers when pearl fishing collapsed and put them in a position to prosper handsomely from the construction boom of the postwar years" (Fred Lawson, *Bahrain: The Modernization of Autocracy* [Boulder: Westview Press], 1989, p. 68).

According to Hooglund, "By 1993 Bahrain's cultivated area had been reduced from 6,000 hectares before independence to 1,500 hectares. The cultivated land consists of about 10,000 plots ranging in size from a few square meters to four hectares. These plots are distributed among approximately 800 owners. A minority of large owners, including individuals and institutions, are absentee landlords who control about 60 percent of all cultivable land. The ruling Al Khalifa own the greatest number of plots, including the largest and most productive ones, although information pertaining to the distribution of ownership among family members is not available" (p. 123).

Political Residency for the Persian Gulf region was moved to Bahrain from Bushehr (Bushire), in Iran, and the Royal Air Force base and Royal Navy facilities on the island assumed greater importance as Britain consolidated its regional forces there. A formal United States military presence in the Persian Gulf also took shape then, with the formation of a three-ship naval task force headquartered at the port of Jufair.[8]

The second defining element is oil. Bahrain was the site of the first commercial oil discovery in the Arabian Peninsula, in 1932. The concession was won by Caltex, a consortium of Texaco and the Standard Oil Company of California (today's Chevron) which established the Bahrain Petroleum Company (BAPCO) as the local operator. Production for export began in 1933, and in 1937 BAPCO opened a large state-of-the-art oil refinery. Bahrain's oil production capacities were always quite modest compared with later finds in the region, but it was here that an oil-based political economy first developed. Oil production and refining led to the growth of ancillary industries and services, and oil revenues allowed for the creation of a modern state apparatus, including the expansion of the first secular educational system in the region. Bahrain was for several decades the main port of entry for eastern Saudi Arabia, and so benefitted from the growth of economic activity that accompanied the subsequent development of the oil industry in that country.

The growth of an administrative apparatus and economic activity powered by the presence of Western oil companies led to the recruitment of labor from outside the island. Educated white-collar workers from the Indian subcontinent, as British subjects until 1947, had an initial advantage, while Omanis, Iranians and others from the immediate environs also responded to the demand for unskilled and semi-skilled workers. More generally, the growth of Bahrain's merchant, service, industrial and administrative sectors led to the development, early compared with the rest of the region, of a relatively differentiated class structure that was reflected in political and trade-union activism to a degree not found elsewhere in the Arabian Peninsula. Finally, the accrual of oil revenues, especially after the major oil companies introduced "profit-sharing" with the producing states' governments in 1950, gave the amir and his entourage a relatively rapid and great advantage of

---

[8] The U.S. naval presence based in Bahrain stood at five ships in the 1970s and early 1980s. Since 1995 Bahrain has been the headquarters of the U.S. Fifth Fleet, and fifteen U.S. warships are presently "home ported" in Bahrain (Anthony H. Cordesman, *Bahrain, Oman, Qatar and the UAE: Challenges of Security* [Boulder: Westview Press, 1997], pp. 38-39).

wealth, enhancing significantly the ruling family's economic autonomy and social power vis-a-vis leading merchant families and other tribal shaikhs.

The combination of foreign (British) political rule and an expanding modern economy and state apparatus produced a political dynamic that more resembled what was happening in Egypt and Iran than elsewhere on the Arab side of the Gulf. Nationalist and pro-independence activism was accompanied by considerable underground trade union activity in sites like the BAPCO refinery, which experienced its first industrial strike in 1943. Serious episodes of political, social and labor unrest, including a dimension of communal conflict between Shi`a and Sunni, erupted on several occasions, beginning in 1953. Shi`a and Sunni community leaders subsequently banded together as the Committee of National Unity (CNU) in 1954, but secret talks between the CNU and the ruling family broke down over "the principle of elections as the legitimate basis for authority."[9] The following several years saw a series of strikes and clashes over a range of local and regional issues and came to a head with the British-French-Israeli Suez invasion in late 1956. The government forcibly suppressed public manifestations of political opposition, and exiled five leaders of the CNU to the island of St. Helena. The government subsequently increased its repressive capabilities by recruiting security personnel from Iraq and elsewhere and setting up a "special branch within the police corps specializing in political affairs," under the command of a seconded British officer.[10] While holding the line against structural reform, the authorities took steps to enhance their political base by decreeing improved working conditions and by conceding a dominant role in the private sector to leading merchant families. When a new wave of labor and political unrest broke out in 1965 over, among other things, the right to unionize and an end to police harassment, the authorities moved quickly to arrest the participants and once again to exile forcibly those it regarded as the leaders.[11]

---

[9] Lawson, p. 63.

[10] Lawson, p. 67. Fred Halliday (*Arabia Without Sultans,* London: Penguin, 1974) notes that "in 1958, out of 60 key posts in the government, 14 were held by Al Khalifa and 23 by British officials," and that "in 1959, out of 739 police, only 202 were Bahrainis. 127 were NorthYemenis, 69 Iraqis, 61 Omanis and an equal number of South Yemenis. Seventeen of the 29 officers were British...."

[11] One legacy of the 1956 upheaval was that the Al Khalifa rulers left their palace in Manama, the capital, and set up permanent residence in the small village of Rifa'a al-Gharb, "which only they and their bedouin guards were permitted to inhabit." See Halliday,

Britain's announcement in 1968 that it would withdraw militarily from and end its direct political role in the Persian Gulf region was accompanied by efforts to forge a political federation of the small amirates it had ruled. The result was the United Arab Emirates, while Bahrain and Qatar opted for independence instead. Bahrain also had to contend with Iranian claims of sovereignty, based on its occupation of the island in the 17th and 18th centuries. A popular referendum would surely have rejected Iran's pretensions, but neither the British nor the Al Khalifa were prepared to entertain such a simple and direct means of gauging political sentiment. Iran's claims were instead neutralized by a March 1970 UN-sponsored "consultation" with, in the words of Secretary-General U Thant's special representative, "organizations and institutions in Bahrain...providing the best and fullest cross-section of opinion among the people of Bahrain."[12] Bahrain became independent on August 16, 1971.

Bahrain's political history, singular in the Gulf, of mass-based movements that cut across class lines and pronounced trade-union activity, required the ruling family to replace the withdrawn colonial power with some form of local legitimacy. Amir Isa, on December 16, 1971, decreed that a national parliament would be formed and announced elections for a Constituent Assembly that would draw up a constitution for the country. The assembly, composed of twenty-two elected and eight appointed members, began its work on December 1, 1972.[13] The resulting

---

p. 445.

A legacy of the 1965 events was the recruitment of Ian Stewart Henderson, a colonial officer who had made his mark in the counterinsurgency war in Kenya. Henderson first served under Chief of Police J.S. Bell as Bell's deputy responsible for the Special Branch. In the 1970s, after independence, Bell became Director General of Public Security, while Henderson served as Bell's assistant director and also as head of the Security and Intelligence Services (SIS), later renamed the State Security Directorate (*Idarat Amn al-Dawla*) but still referred to by most Bahrainis as the SIS. In 1992, when Bell retired, Henderson took over as director general of the Public Security Directorate, the Criminal Investigations Directorate (CID), and the State Security Directorate.

[12] This process has frequently and incorrectly been referred to as a "referendum" (see, for example, Cordesman, p. 41). The list contained "not a single trades union or political party" (Halliday, p. 457).

[13] Labor unrest broke out in March 1972, and in September of that year there was a general strike in support of airport construction site workers. In addition, there was "considerable underground activity" by cadres of the Popular Front for the Liberation of Bahrain. This was the local organization of what had been, until 1968, the Arab Nationalist

document, promulgated in June 1973, provided for a National Assembly of thirty elected members and up to fourteen cabinet members serving *ex officio*. The assembly was not authorized to initiate legislation but could question the government about existing or proposed legislation and projects.[14] National elections were held on December 7, 1973, and the constitution went into effect with the first meeting of the National Assembly, on December 16, 1973.[15]

Political parties remained illegal, and candidates ran as independents, but three relatively distinct groupings emerged from the first campaign and functioning of the assembly: a People's Bloc of eight leftist and Arab nationalist candidates with ties to underground and transnational parties such as the Communists (the National Liberation Front) and the Arab Nationalist Movement (the Popular Front for the Liberation of Bahrain); a Religious Bloc of six, mainly teachers and religious court judges based in rural Shi`a constituencies; and an Independent Middle—sixteen in number—not bound to either of the other blocs organizationally or ideologically and representing "a varying combination of wealth, education, family preeminence, government contacts, and the ability to employ or affect the employment of people."[16] The fourteen appointed cabinet members had the same rights and privileges as the elected members, which meant that the government could gain majority approval of any motion or legislation with the support of fewer than one-third of the elected members, though in practice it preferred to secure an elected majority.

Movement and was known until 1974 as the Popular Front for the Liberation of Oman and the Arab Gulf (PFLOAG) (see Halliday, p. 460).

[14] Article 35 of the constitution states, "The Amir shall have the right to initiate laws, and he alone shall ratify and promulgate the laws." Article 42 states, "No law may be promulgated unless it has been passed by the National Assembly and ratified by the Amir." Article 43, specifying the composition of the assembly, states that the number of elected members will increase to forty in the election to the second four-year term.

[15] The electorate was restricted to native-born male citizens twenty years of age and older (see Hooglund, pp. 137-39).

[16] "Because of its variation and political heterogeneity, the Independent Middle was never able to operate as a united bloc save when the national policy of free market and enterprise was in question.... [T]hey were sarcastically and conventionally known as the government bloc...[although] [i]t happened several times that members of the Independent Middle voted down officially proposed legislation, most notable of which was the State of Emergency Law of 1974...." (Khuri, p. 229).

Bahrain's experiment in quasi-representative political participation lasted less than two years. "Many people felt emboldened," one activist of the period told Human Rights Watch:

> Women's groups were circulating petitions demanding their rights, and conservative mullahs were collecting signatures demanding gender segregation in public spaces and government institutions. Clubs were organizing classes on managing strikes and labor negotiations. From the government's perspective, the situation was getting out of hand.[17]

In October 1974, following a period that also saw numerous strikes at the Aluminum Bahrain (ALBA) plant, the Bahrain drydocks, Gulf Air, and many less prominent establishments, Amir Isa decreed a broadly written State Security Measures Law (generally referred to as the State Security Law) that would allow the government to arrest and imprison for up to three years without trial any person suspected of having "perpetrated acts, delivered statements, exercised activities or [...] been involved in contacts inside or outside the country, which are of a nature considered to be in violation of the internal or external security of the country...."[18]

---

[17] Communication (May 5, 1997) from Abd al-Hadi Khalaf, now a sociologist living in involuntary exile (see below). "I'm sure the U.S. did not like the debate in and outside the parliament concerning the government plan to renew its naval base rental agreement," Khalaf added.

[18] The decree states (Article 6) that "All persons who are committed to specified prisons in implementation of detention orders issued pursuant to Public Security Order No.1 are considered to be detained under this law." It further provides that anyone so detained may submit a complaint three months after arrest to the High Court of Appeal sitting in special sessions which are held *in camera.* The law states that the court may set its own procedures "without observing the [due process] procedures stipulated in the [1966] Law of Criminal Procedures." The complaint, if it is rejected, may be renewed at six-month intervals (see below, note 90). The decree does not indicate that detainees must be informed of this right of complaint. It does state, however, that there should be only one copy of the proceedings which cannot be reproduced and which together with all depositions, are deposited under seal with the court. The decree also stipulates that the minister of interior immediately be sent a copy of the judgment. Bahrain's Interior Ministry, in a November 1992 compilation of this and other security decrees, characterized the decree as "an exceedingly valuable counter terrorist measure" that was "especially useful in the turbulent times of the late 70s and early 80s when rapid and effective action was needed to insure calm in the community."

Many in the National Assembly demanded that it be submitted for approval or modification before implementation. The government, bearing in mind the many formal protests and petitions previously submitted requesting suspension of the 1965 Public Security Law, was unwilling to do this. In the subsequent months of behind-the-scenes bargaining, the government was unable to split the alliance of the People's Bloc, the Religious Bloc, and many of the Independent Middle on this issue. "The longer the issue persisted in public and the longer the debates continued," Khuri writes, "the weaker the government's position became."[19] In May 1975, the government unilaterally withdrew from a session scheduled to discuss the measures. In August 1975, when it appeared that the summer recess had not changed the dynamics, the government dissolved the National Assembly.[20] When Minister of Information Muhammad Ibrahim al-Mutawa'a was asked in early 1996 why the National Assembly had been disbanded, he replied that it had

---

According to Lawson (p. 84), the decree manifests the ascendancy of the hard-line views of the prime minister, the amir's brother, on the issue of how to respond to labor and political unrest. For an account of the ALBA strike and other labor initiatives at the time, see Abd al-Hadi Khalaf, "Labor Movements in Bahrain," *MERIP Reports* #132 (May 1985), p. 26.

[19] Khuri, a Lebanese anthropologist, was living in Bahrain and conducting field research at the time. "The issue of public security and state of emergency, the subject of many formal protests since 1956, was suddenly brought back to life, becoming the concern of a large part of Bahraini society. Many panels in clubs, editorials in the daily press, and person-to-person conversations centered on this law.... Many parliamentarians in the independent middle, who would not have cared either way, succumbed to social pressure and pledged in public to vote against the law if it was submitted unmodified to the parliament" (p. 232).

[20] Article 65 of the constitution states the Amir may dissolve the assembly "by a decree in which the reasons for dissolution shall be indicated," but further states that "elections for the new Assembly shall be held within a period not exceeding two months from the date of dissolution," and that "[i]f the elections are not held within the said period, the dissolved Assembly shall be restored to its full constitutional authority and shall meet immediately as if the dissolution had not taken place...[and] shall then continue functioning until a new Assembly is elected." By the terms of its own constitution, then, the government of Bahrain has been operating outside the law since October 1975.

"hindered the government," and that it would be restored "[o]nce we feel that we need it, when it is suitable for our society and development."[21]

In March 1976, in the spirit of the State Security Measures Law, the government replaced the penal code of 1955 and separately decreed what has come to be known as the State Security Court to try those accused of violating those articles relating to internal and external security.[22] The government also followed its dissolution of the National Assembly with a wave of arrests, detentions without trial, and forced exile that by the end of the decade had crippled the leftist and secular nationalist opposition. This opposition, with its base in the trade union movement, was also undermined in the 1980s by socioeconomic changes that included a shift from manufacturing to services, in particular offshore banking and tourism, and a great increase in the numbers and proportion of foreign workers.[23]

The 1978-79 revolution in Iran, meanwhile, mobilized a different sort of opposition, one rooted in the majority Shi`a community which expressed itself in religious language and responded enthusiastically to the Ayatollah Khomeini's

---

[21] Reuter, January 17, 1996. A leading Bahraini businessman in Manama, in a conversation with Human Rights Watch in June 1996 about the movement to restore the parliament, cited Bahrain's 85 percent literacy rate and its long-standing modern educational system to support his claim that a constitution and "rule of law" was appropriate for Bahrain. "The man who brought us our drinks," he said, referring to an Indian house servant, "he can vote for a parliament, but I can't!"

[22] Amiri Decree 7/1976 ("Concerning the Formation and Procedures with Respect to Court Provided for in Article 185 of the Penal Code") specifies that "the Civil High Court of Appeal, consisting of three judges, shall be the court competent to look into crimes provided for in Articles 112 to 184 [comprising the chapters on external and internal security and on demonstrations and riots] of the Penal Code of 1976, as per Article 185 of the Penal Code." In deference to common usage, including that of the government of Bahrain, this report refers to this court in this function as the State Security Court, although it has not been formally designated as such. The High Court of Appeal also hears wrongful detention complaints from those detained under the State Security Measures Law (see above, note 18), but this function is separate again from its sitting as the so-called State Security Court.

[23] The offshore banking boom accompanied the sharp rise in oil revenues between 1974 and 1980. According to Khalaf, "State expenditures increased tenfold from BD 33 million in 1972 to BD 348 million in 1980.... [enabling the government] to reduce some sources of popular discontent, particularly in the public services and housing sectors" (p. 27). Khalaf also notes that non-Bahrainis comprised 32 percent of the population in 1981, nearly double the 17.5 percent of a decade earlier.

identification of Shi`a populations as among the dispossessed of the earth. The early demands of this opposition to establish an Islamic republic alienated leftist and nationalist opposition elements among the Sunnis and many secularist Shi`a as well. This specifically Shi`a opposition manifested itself in specific organizational forms, notably the Islamic Front for the Liberation of Bahrain, but also in a more generalized sense of a community with multiple grievances against a government that it perceived as having a strong sectarian animus with regard to their well-being and empowerment. In December 1981, the government arrested some seventy-three persons, mostly Bahrainis but including several Shi`a from Saudi Arabia and elsewhere in the region, on charges of plotting, with assistance from Iran, to overthrow the state.[24] Following several months of incommunicado detention and alleged torture, and amendments to key security clauses of the 1976 Penal Code that retroactively permitted the government to try all of the accused before the State Security Court, the defendants went on trial in March 1982; in May three were sentenced to life in prison, fifty-nine received sentences of fifteen years, and ten were sentenced to seven years.[25]

Over subsequent years the government continued to imprison and exile opposition activists, religious and leftist alike. Many Bahrainis who went abroad to study became engaged in Bahraini and pan-Arab organizations that the government regarded as hostile, and were subsequently refused permission to re-enter the country. The Al Khalifa family continued to monopolize political power; the cabinet or council of ministers selected by Amir Isa in 1971 included seven members of the Al Khalifa family. While there have been occasional resignations of individual ministers over the intervening two decades, June 1995 was the first time since independence in 1971 that the prime minister and the full cabinet

---

[24] Those arrested were fifty-eight Bahrainis, thirteen Saudis, one Kuwaiti and one Omani. Some 300 Bahrainis, at least some of whom were *biduun* (without nationality) of Iranian origin, were forcibly exiled. For a summary account that largely reflects the perspective of the Bahraini government, see Cordesman, p. 42-43. One Bahraini living in exile told Human Rights Watch that the authorities deported many residents, while others left out of fear of being detained on the basis of confessions of those in detention. In addition, others were encouraged to leave for Iran by Shaikh Hadi al-Mudaressi, head of the Islamic Front (written communication, May 1997).

[25] The amended articles, published in the Official Gazette no. 1477 (March 4, 1982), allow the government to prosecute a defendant or defendants before the State Security Court rather than the ordinary criminal court as long as at least one of the charges against at least one of the codefendants comes under the jurisdiction of the security court.

resigned. In the new cabinet, however, the premiership and the major portfolios remained in the hands of the same members of the ruling family.

4. ORIGINS OF THE PRESENT CRISIS

In the period immediately after the Gulf War, many Bahrainis discerned an opportunity to press for political liberalization. In discussions with Human Rights Watch, a number of Bahraini reform activists cited as inspiration the broad movement among Kuwaitis to demand political reforms, including elections and the reestablishment of the parliament disbanded there in 1986. Even in Saudi Arabia, petitions to the royal family from liberals and Islamists alike demanded political accountability and an end to corruption. Outside the region, the demise of the Soviet Union removed a longstanding anti-communist rationale for repressive policies. A related external development was the prominence of "democratization" as a policy theme among Western governments, notably the United States, and U.S. pressures on the Kuwaiti ruling family—though decidedly not on their Saudi or Bahraini counterparts—to countenance elections and to halt egregious civil rights abuses. In the words of one reformist lawyer:

> [Bahrain's] 1973 constitution represented a compromise, a contract. It legitimizes the Al Khalifa as the ruling family. There were long discussions in the Constituent Assembly. The conservatives wanted any National Assembly to be appointed. The liberals wanted all the members to be elected. What we produced was a reasonable compromise. Ideal, in fact. It placed restrictions on the amir while preserving many of his prerogatives. It fit perfectly the Bahrain mix.[26]

While hostile to those citizens campaigning for political reforms, the Al Khalifas appreciated the need for gestures that would counter the erosion of legitimacy visited on the Gulf ruling families by the Iraqi invasion of Kuwait and all that followed. In April 1992, for instance, the government informally sent out

---

[26] Human Rights Watch interview, Manama, June 1996. This is a view that seems to be shared broadly but not completely by the opponents of the government. The main exception is the Islamic Front for the Liberation of Bahrain, whose spokespersons told Human Rights Watch that their goal was to replace the monarchy with a republican form of government—though not, they insisted, an Islamic republic as in Iran (Human Rights Watch interviews, London, March 1996, and Beirut, May 1996). At the time, in 1973, the Popular Front opposed the constitution and parliamentary elections as insufficiently revolutionary, and held that only armed struggle could bring about needed political change.

word that some 120 Bahrainis living in exile would be allowed to return.[27] The next month, on the occasion of Id al-Fitr, a holiday when Muslim rulers customarily issue pardons or reduce sentences, Amir Isa pardoned a number of prisoners, although it is not known if these pardons included persons jailed for political offenses. In May 1992 the government reportedly took steps, despite its own budgetary difficulties, to increase housing and utility subsidies as a move to address the growing complaints of the mostly Shi`a poor.

The Petition Campaign
The government's gestures stopped well short of any endorsement of political reform that would compromise the ruling family's absolute authority. Precisely such reforms and compromises, however, comprised the agendas of the country's political intelligentsia, particularly the issue of how to build momentum toward restoration of the National Assembly and parliamentary elections. Beginning in the early months of 1991, these themes were discussed in regular informal meetings in people's houses, since public gatherings to discuss politics were outlawed. "I was among fifteen or so persons who gathered together to discuss how to reactivate the constitution," one professional told Human Rights Watch. "Some of these meetings were at my home. Many people started to come."[28] "Concentric discussion circles" was how another participant characterized the process. "Out of those discussions we set up a committee structure to move things ahead more effectively."[29]
A formal petition was drawn up by late October 1992. After an initial signing at the home of Ali Rabi`a, a prominent leftist and former elected member of the National Assembly, it was circulated privately and soon secured more than 280 signatures of merchants, lawyers, writers, and other professionals, including several former elected members of parliament. "It was pretty much restricted to the

---

[27] Ambassador Abdul Ghaffar, in his letter to Human Rights Watch, asserted that "the alleged exile of political opponents is a non-issue" and that "a previous issue of disaffected Bahrainis...was fully resolved by many of those returning under a Government plan during 1992-94." One Bahraini lawyer characterized those invited to return as "second and third class opponents." No prominent opposition figures who attempted to return, religious or secularist, were allowed to do so (see below). Human Rights Watch interview, December 1996.

[28] Human Rights Watch interview, Manama, June 1996.

[29] Human Rights Watch interview, Manama, June 1996.

intelligentsia," one of those involved told Human Rights Watch, "but at that level most sectors were engaged." The petition, about two pages long, praised the amir's "pioneering" role in promulgating the 1973 constitution and requested that he "issue orders for election of the National Assembly as outlined by section two of chapter four of the constitution."[30] "We paid our full respects to the amir," one participant told Human Rights Watch. "We are not a very aggressive opposition."[31]

The government's response was ambivalent. Initially the government moved to preempt and coopt those demanding restoration of the National Assembly by appointing a thirty-person Consultative Council, or Shura Council, whose main function would be to "comment" on legislation proposed by the government-appointed cabinet. "The shura proposal was 95 percent made-in-Saudi Arabia," one Bahraini businessman-reformer told Human Rights Watch. "Even those cabinet ministers who were not Al Khalifa were very surprised when it was announced."[32] The November 1992 petition concluded by acknowledging the ruler's right to establish such a body, but declared that it "does not replace the national assembly as a constitutional and legislative authority."[33]

Some of those involved in the petition campaign had considered it imperative to present the petition to the amir before the expected proclamation of the Shura Council, while others counseled a more patient approach in which "acceptable liberals" rather than high-profile long-time critics would take the lead. In the end, those favoring a preemptive approach carried the day. On November 15, 1992, a six-member delegation comprising three Sunni and three Shi`a leaders—conservative Shi`a jurist and community leader Shaikh Abd al-Amir al-Jamri; Abd al-Wahab Hussain Ali, a teacher and leading Shi`a activist; Shaikh Abd al-Latif al-Mahmud, a leading Sunni reformist theologian; Muhammad Jabr al-Sabah, a former member of parliament; Shaikh Isa al-Jawdar, a prominent conservative Sunni personality; and Hamid Sanghur, a prominent Shi`a lawyer—met with Amir Isa. Of these, only Sanghur, a former head of the Bahrain Bar Association and since deceased, was not associated with dissenting political

---

[30] "The Historic Petition: Translation of the Petition Submitted to the Amir of Bahrain on 15 November 1992," provided electronically by the Bahrain Freedom Movement (London).

[31] Human Rights Watch interview, Manama, June 1996.

[32] Human Rights Watch interview, November 1996.

[33] "The Historic Petition."

forces. Their reception, it seems, was frosty, and the meeting was brief. "The amir told us he was about to initiate the Shura Council and that was all we could expect," one of those involved in the campaign told Human Rights Watch.[34] "Despite several calls we made to the Amiri Court over many months, we never got an official response," said another.[35] This was one of the only times that the ruler met with a delegation that included both Shi`a and Sunni figures. In subsequent requests by citizens for meetings, the amir has reportedly insisted on meeting separately with Sunni and Shi`a delegations. Critics say that this is one way in which the government exacerbates communal divisions.

On December 16, 1992, Bahrain's national day, Amir Isa announced the appointed Shura Council, which held its first meeting in January 1993. The thirty council members, appointed for a term of four years, were mostly businessmen, but the group included lawyers and judges as well as several ex-members of the dissolved National Assembly. The first chair was Minister of Transport Ibrahim Humaydan. All council meetings are closed to the public and no transcripts are made available. The amir, in a November 1993 interview, characterized the council as a forum for "serious discussion." Its activities, he said, were "distinguished by civilized debate, best reflected in a democratic dialogue...and in mutual understanding between the government and the council."[36] Among the dozens of interviews that Human Rights Watch conducted among Bahraini business and professional people, however, not one person considered the Consultative Council to represent a serious or sincere gesture of reform. Most Bahrainis who spoke with Human Rights Watch, including one former cabinet member, said that even the cabinet itself was no longer the site of useful policy discussion, and in recent years assembled only to rubber-stamp the decisions of Prime Minister Khalifa bin Salman Al Khalifa, the brother of the amir, and to hear from a small number of other influential officials, most notably Minister of Interior Muhammad bin Khalifa

---

[34] Human Rights Watch interview, Manama, June 1996. According to the *Middle East Contemporary Survey* [*MECS*], the November 1992 petition had been "signed by over 150 public figures representing most of the ideological and political movements in the country" (*MECS 1992* [Tel Aviv: Dayan Center, 1995] p. 361). Human Rights Watch interviewed several signatories, all of whom agree that the number was in the range of 300.

[35] Human Rights Watch interview, Manama, June 1996.

[36] The interview, in the London-based Arabic daily *Al-Hawadith*, is cited in *MECS 1993* (Tel Aviv, 1995), p. 278.

Al Khalifa, a first cousin of the amir. This skeptical Bahraini view of the Shura Council stands in contrast to much more positive assessments, both public and private, by Bahrain's allies, notably the United States government.[37]

In 1993-1994, as the political crisis continued to simmer, Bahrain's economy remained stagnant. The economic downturn in the region generally, and in Saudi Arabia in particular, reduced overall economic activity and cash transfers to Bahrain from wealthier neighbor governments. In real terms the country's gross domestic product contracted by 1.8 percent in 1994, and another one percent in 1995.[38] Official unemployment climbed to 15 percent overall, and was estimated to be twice that rate among young men in Shi`a communities, as the growth in the number of jobs failed to keep pace with the growth of the labor force.[39] Growth in employment of non-Bahrainis continued to exceed that of Bahrainis, despite government promises to restrict the number of new work permits.[40]

Several of those in the reformist camp told Human Rights Watch that they continued to be in contact with high-level government officials during this period. The prime minister, for example, conducted regular Wednesday evening informal gatherings—sometimes inviting bankers and economists, for instance, or on another occasion lawyers and judges—to which government critics were occasionally invited as well.

---

[37] President Clinton, for instance, in a June 1996 letter to Amir Isa, praised the ruler's decision to expand the Shura Council to forty members as a reaffirmation of Bahrain's commitment to "economic and social development and political reconciliation." U.S. State Department officials who monitor for Bahrain have indicated to Human Rights Watch that they consider the Shura Council to represent a serious effort at political reform.

[38] Economist Intelligence Unit, *Bahrain*, 2nd Quarter 1995, p. 6.

[39] *Financial Times*, March 16, 1995; "The Two Worlds of Bahrain: Shiite Majority Wants Its Share of Sunni-Ruled Island's Prosperity," *Washington Post*, June 13, 1995, p. A15.

[40] According to official census data, between 1981 and 1991, out of 74,200 new jobs in the economy, 54,100 were filled by expatriates. Of the 20,100 filled by Bahrainis, 15,800 were with the government and only 4,300 in the private sector (D.F. Hepburn, "Bahrain Economy," prepared for the National Council for U.S.-Arab Relations, March 18, 1996, pp. 10-11). A plan announced in 1989 to shift 20,000 jobs from expatriates to Bahrainis by the end of 1995 had in fact found only 8,543 jobs by that date, according to the Ministry of Labor and Social Affairs.

Demonstrations

In 1994, economic and political discontent moved from the living rooms and offices of the elite to the streets. In mid-January 1994, security forces forcibly dispersed a memorial service at Mu'min mosque, in central Manama, commemorating the fortieth day since the death of Sayyid Mohammed Reza Golpayegani, a leading Iranian Shi`a jurist and at the time one of Shi`ism's five "great ayatollahs."[41] One of those scheduled to speak at the service was Shaikh Ali Salman, a young Bahraini cleric who had studied in Qom. Salman told Human Rights Watch that Bahraini authorities typically required official authorization for events of this sort, but that just as typically permission was not sought and that enforcement was erratic. On this occasion, up to a thousand persons gathered on the evening of January 19. According to Salman, no one considered it especially unusual or ominous that security forces had surrounded the mosque.[42] What followed, however, was a confrontation unusual for its violence. One young man who had attended told Human Rights Watch that about one hour after the service started, following Salman's remarks, the security forces announced over loudspeakers that everyone had to leave within the next five minutes.

> But before the five minutes were up, they shot a tear gas canister into the mosque. Then they threw in a lot of tear gas. People panicked. Shaikh Ali had urged us not to go outside, not to push the government. But because of the gas we had to get out. When we went outside, we threw stones at the police, and they shot tear gas back at us. Cars followed us out of Manama. Maybe two dozen people were arrested.[43]

---

[41] Yann Richard, in *Shi'ite Islam* (Oxford: Blackwell, 1995), characterizes Golpayegani as a theologian "who had resisted the revolutionary wave [in Iran] and had maintained a profound following among the people," (p. 84).

[42] Human Rights Watch interview, London, March 1996. A Bahraini lawyer told Human Rights Watch that since the early 1980s security forces have frequently intervened to prevent or to disperse religious gatherings. "The Shi`a have some thirty very public rituals each year," this person said. "In times of crisis, these become occasions to express themselves together. But the occasions themselves are traditional" (interview, December 1996).

[43] Human Rights Watch interview, Kuwait, May 1996.

According to a brief Reuter account based on interviews after the event with eyewitnesses, "at some stage the security forces fired numerous rounds of tear gas into the open area outside the mosque building," arrested about two dozen people, and subsequently sealed the area and shut the mosque.[44]

Several persons recalled to Human Rights Watch that 1994 was characterized by "an overbearing sense of stagnation" that was economic as well as political. Ministers spoke of "greater economic opportunities," but unemployment continued to worsen. That summer witnessed several large demonstrations of young men at the Ministry of Labor, in Isa Town. The first, on June 29, ended "amicably" when the 200 or so youths present were told to return on July 2 to register as job-seekers. When 1,500 showed up and tried to organize a sit-in, riot police were called in and tear gas was used to disperse the crowd. The similar sequence occurred on August 31 and September 3.[45] Several arrests were made, including Shaikh Ali Salman, who told Human Rights Watch that he had been involved in organizing the demonstrations. He was detained and questioned by security forces for a day and had his passport confiscated.[46]

Political frustrations were also mounting, as the campaign to restore the parliament encountered continued government intransigence. Some of the organizers of the 1992 petition effort initiated a second, "popular" version. which retained the focus of the first but spoke more critically of the economic crisis and of "laws which were enacted during the absence of the parliament which restrict the freedom of citizens and contradict the Constitution."[47] The second petition also

---

[44] Reuter, January 24, 1994. The Reuter account also reproduced the ambiguous justification of the government in writing that "hundreds of people had apparently gathered illegally" and that "this had been an unauthorized gathering." Article 178 of the 1976 Penal Code proscribes gatherings of five or more persons "with the aim of committing crimes...[or] undermining public security," and Article 180 authorizes the use of "force within reasonable limits" to disperse such gatherings. The Bahraini authorities have used these provisions to deny citizens the right of peaceful assembly, in violation of Article 28 of Bahrain's constitution (see below) and in contravention of Article 20 of the Universal Declaration of Human Rights. Police intervention in the case of religious gatherings, however, had been inconsistent.

[45] Reuter, September 4, 1994.

[46] Human Rights Watch interview, London, March 1996.

[47] English text from Bahrain Freedom Movement, Voice of Bahrain homepage (http:// ourworld.compuserve.com/ homepages/Bahrain).

called for "the involvement of women in the democratic process." Munira Fakhro, a professor of sociology at the University of Bahrain and one of the country's most prominent women professionals, was among the fourteen original signatories.[48] Within a month, the organizers claimed, between 20,000 and 25,000 signatures had been gathered. But whereas the signatories to the first petition were more or less evenly divided between Sunni and Shi`a, the tens of thousands of signatories to the "popular petition" were overwhelmingly Shi`a, reflecting the strong sense of oppression and alienation felt by many Bahraini Shi`a and the active role of young Shi`a clerics, including Ali Salman, in promoting the campaign in sermons and in meetings in various *ma'tam*s.[49] Many of those associated with the first petition also endorsed the second, although some considered it a strategic error to take the campaign for political reform to the street, thereby allowing the regime to portray it as a sectarian movement pitting Shi`a against Sunni, and to invoke in the process a "foreign threat"—i.e., Iranian support for opposition activity by Bahrain's Shi`a majority.

On November 25, 1994, a confrontation occurred around a marathon relay race involving Bahrainis and Western expatriates alike that was a vehicle for raising funds for charities. On this occasion, the route of the race ran through several Shi`a villages in the vicinity of the capital.[50] A group of Shi`a young men

---

[48] The campaign to gather signatures began with a public meeting on September 26, 1994, at the home of Shaikh Abd al-Amir al Jamri. The other original signatories, in addition to al-Jamri and Fakhro, were Abd al-Latif al-Mahmud, Muhammad Jabr al-Sabah, Isa al-Jawdar, Ahmad al-Shamlan, Abd al-Wahab Hussain, Ali Qassim Rabi`a, Hisham al-Shihabi, Abd al-Aziz Hasan Ubol, Ibrahim Sayyid Ali Kamal al-Din, Sa`id al-Asboul, Abdallah al-Abbasi, and Abdallah Rashid.

[49] Often translated in English as "funeral homes," these are spaces of Shi`a congregation for worship as well as for funerals, weddings, and preparation for the annual procession for `ashura, commemorating the martyrdom of Imam Ali in the first Islamic century. Along with the mosque, they have served as a locale for barely disguised Shi`a opposition political organizing, and have been the target of disruptive attacks by state security forces.

[50] The race has frequently been referred to as an annual event, although according to one long-time Western resident who had participated in earlier relays, the last time it had been run was in 1986 or 1987. As this person put it, while Bahrain's small size "made it hard to have a seventy-five-kilometer race that did not go into Shi`a neighborhoods," it was also well known that these socially very conservative villages posed a certain risk. "I thought

organized a protest, reportedly citing the participation of some Western women in running attire, which they considered to be an affront to local mores. The demonstrators held up protest signs, shouted slogans, and reportedly threw stones at the runners. According to Shaikh Ali Salman, whom the government later accused of fomenting the confrontation:

> About a hundred youths went out for an hour to protest. They took banners to protest the race. They were dispersed about 1:30 p.m. The government says the youths threw stones. Maybe, but not enough to keep the marathon from proceeding to the Diplomat Hotel back in Manama, where it ended around 5 p.m.[51]

According to Salman, some twenty young men were arrested that night; about ten were released about two weeks later, but nine were still in detention in mid-1996, nearly a year and a half later.[52] Salman was himself arrested on December 5, 1994, at his home in Bilad al-Qadim, allegedly for inciting the marathon incident and then organizing protests against the arrests that followed.

The arrest and detention of Ali Salman sparked fierce protests and street clashes throughout the heavily-populated environs of Manama and Sitra in December 1994 and January 1995. According to the Ministry of Interior, which generally played down the extent of the disturbances in the period leading up to the mid-December Gulf Cooperation Council (GCC) ministerial conference, demonstrations occurred practically on a daily basis.[53] As clashes escalated, some demonstrations involved attacks with crude petrol bombs on police stations, banks and commercial properties. On December 12, security forces sealed off the neighborhoods of Bilad al-Qadim and al-Mukharga. Security forces employed

---

they were nuts to go through those villages the way they did," this person told Human Rights Watch.

[51] Human Rights Watch interview, London, March 1996.

[52] Human Rights Watch interview, London, March 1996. It is not known if those persons are still in detention at the time of writing.

[53] The first official comment on the demonstrations was an Interior Ministry statement sent to Reuter, which said that a runner had been injured in the marathon incident and that an investigation had "established that [Salman] was the mastermind and organizer of these events" (Reuter, December 17, 1994).

rubber bullets as well as tear gas canisters fired at street level and from helicopters.[54] In Sanabis, use of live ammunition by security forces was apparently responsible for the deaths of Hani Abbas Khamis and Hani Ahmad al-Wasti. During December another civilian and one policeman were also killed. The U.S. Embassy estimated that by the end of December the authorities had detained between 500 and 600 persons, and several hundred more in January.[55] In addition to those rounded up in the street, scores more were seized by security forces in raids on homes in Diraz, Sitra, Sanabis, Jidd Hafs, Da`ir and elsewhere.

In a December 1994 meeting with a group of four Shi`a community leaders seeking Salman's release, the minister of interior asserted that the government had confessions and incriminating documents that confirmed Salman's instigatory role in the political turbulence. According to one participant, the minister of interior told the group that the government would not free Salman but would put him on trial and prove the charges.[56] On January 15, 1995, however, the government announced it had that day forcibly exiled a group of "infiltrators who

---

[54] For an account of early demonstrations, for the most part reflecting the government's perspective, see Reuter, December 17, 1994. A longtime Western resident in Bahrain who lived in the vicinity of Bani Jamra during the time in question told Human Rights Watch that on several occasions he had witnessed helicopters firing projectiles into villages (interview, London, June 1996). According to *The Military Balance, 1995-1996*, the Bahraini Ministry of Interior possesses two Hughes 500, two Bell 412 and one Bell 205 helicopters; this is in addition to seventeen helicopters with the Bahrain Defense Forces.

Rubber bullets, intended as a less lethal alternative to live ammunition, can also be deadly, depending on the type used and the distance from which they are fired. Rubber bullets used (and made) in Israel, for instance, are half-inch metal or hard rubber pellets coated in plastic or rubber, which can pierce flesh at a range of about eighty feet. The Israeli human rights organization B'Tselem reports that rubber bullets have been responsible for more than forty Palestinian fatalities since 1987, including two in April 1997 ("Israel Rubber Bullets Claim Victims," Associated Press, April 12, 1997).

[55] U.S. Department of State, "Bahrain," *Country Reports on Human Rights Practices for 1995* (Washington: U.S. Government Printing Office, March 1996), p. 1056.

[56] Interview with Shaikh Khalil Sultan, Beirut, May 1996. According to Shaikh Khalil, the others in the meeting were Shaikh Hamza al-Dairi, subsequently expelled with Shaikh Ali, and two "non-political" figures, Shaikh Ahmad Asfur and Shaikh Sulaiman al-Medeni. "Our agenda was to free Ali Salman," Shaikh Khalil told Human Rights Watch. "We did not discuss the parliament, the constitution, or anything else."

were inciting sabotage."[57] These were Salman and two other young clerics, Shaikh Hamza al-Dairi and Shaikh Haidar al-Sitri, who had been arrested in late December. Shaikh Adil al-Shu'la, age twenty-eight, was arrested on January 7, 1995, and forcibly exiled to Syria on January 18. According to Amnesty International, Shaikh Muhammad Kojestah and two other persons were also forcibly exiled in January 1995.

The Government's Response

December 1994 saw the outbreak of protracted social unrest that, with some lapses, is now in its third year. In the months following December 1994 there were continued street protests, further arrests, and several government announcements of prisoner releases. In late February 1995, the prime minister stated that 300 persons remained in detention in connection with the unrest, while Reuter cited local resident estimates of around 2,000.[58] In March and April the number of incidents and arrests climbed again, and there were additional fatalities. While some of those arrested were picked up for specific offenses involving violence or vandalism, and some for nonviolent activities such as distributing leaflets, writing graffiti or publicly urging the government to negotiate with the opposition, many arrests were indiscriminate and many of those detained were never formally charged.

Among those held without charges were the most politically prominent detainees, such as Shaikh Abd al-Amir al-Jamri, an elected member of the dissolved National Assembly and the informal head of the most broadly based opposition grouping, the Bahrain Islamic Freedom Movement.[59] He was detained on April 1, 1995, along with several other Shi`a community leaders, including Abd al-Wahab Hussain, Hasan Mushaima, and Shaikh Khalil Sultan. "We were not

---

[57] Reuter, January 18, 1995. The government reportedly asserts that Salman had been deported some years earlier, had been allowed to re-enter the country only after signing a statement agreeing to desist from political activity, and by his speeches and activism in the petition campaign had violated that agreement (Cordesman, p. 81).

[58] Reuter, March 3, 1995.

[59] The group calls itself the Bahrain Freedom Movement in English, but its formal name in Arabic is Harakat Ahrar al-Bahrain al-Islamiyya. According to persons in the exile leadership, this reflects an internal "compromise" between traditional and modern political elements in the Freedom Movement, which characterizes itself as a "tendency" rather than as a party or an organization. This report includes "Islamic" in the name when referring to the Bahrain-based component of the movement.

surprised when they took us," Shaikh Khalil told Human Rights Watch. "We knew they were recording our sermons."[60] At no point in the ensuing five months of captivity were any of the detained community leaders charged with a crime.[61]

Very soon, though, the authorities engaged them in jailhouse negotiations. "The negotiations started sometime in May," Shaikh Khalil told Human Rights Watch, "and later that month they agreed to put us together in the same *mukhabarat* [intelligence services] prison." According to Shaikh Khalil, between May and August there were about twenty meetings of an hour or two each with Ian Henderson, director of the government's security and investigative directorates, or one of his deputies, Adil Flaifil, and several meetings with the minister of interior.[62] "They were very inconsistent," Shaikh Khalil told Human Rights Watch. "First they'd assert that our arrest had calmed things down, then they'd say we would have to promise to calm things down in order to get out. They kept insisting we were 'nobodies,' and so they were reluctant to acknowledge that we could calm things down." In mid-August, according to Shaikh Khalil and other opposition sources, an understanding seemed to have been reached whereby the opposition would cease street protests, and the government would take steps toward satisfying the demands to reinstate the constitution and restore the national assembly, release political prisoners, and allow exiles to return. At the government's insistence, though, according to Shaikh Khalil, nothing was committed to paper, and

---

[60] Human Rights Watch interview, Beirut, May 1996.

[61] Shaikh al-Jamri was initially placed under house arrest, along with numerous members of his family, in a raid by security forces that left at least one person in his village dead and sixteen injured. After several weeks he was taken to an undisclosed military location. British officials, in a communication to Lord Eric Avebury, chair of the Parliamentary Human Rights Group, on July 21, 1995, wrote: "The Bahraini authorities wish to assure you that Sheikh al-Jamri is fully aware of the specific reasons for his detention. They have informed us that he is being detained under Section 1 of the Detention Order [presumably referring to the 1974 State Security Measures Law], which is subject to regular judicial review, and that the case is a matter of the highest national security for the Bahraini Government." (Letter from Lynda Chalker, Minister of State with the Foreign and Commonwealth Office, reprinted in *Bahrain: A Brickwall* [London; Parliamentary Human Rights Group, 1996].)

[62] Henderson (see above, note 11) reports officially to the minister of interior, and his offices are in the large ministry compound in central Manama which also serves as the country's main detention and interrogation center. He reputedly also has direct access to the prime minister and to Amir Isa.

independent opposition figures subsequently told Human Rights Watch that the government in fact did not go beyond promising to "look into" these demands. Shaikh Khalil and Hasan Mushaima were released then on the understanding that they would travel to Damascus and London to persuade exiled regime opponents to end their activities. Abd al-Wahab Hussain was released on September 9, and Shaikh al-Jamri on September 26. There were also releases of persons rounded up in arrest sweeps at various points over the previous nine months.[63]

Street protests diminished for a time, but the regime's opponents soon charged that the government was not acting in good faith. The government denied that there had been any understanding, and the situation quickly deteriorated. By December, after the High Court of Appeal upheld the death sentence against a man convicted of killing a security officer, street protests and widespread arrests resumed.[64] Shaikh al-Jamri and other Shi`a leaders, in their sermons, resumed criticism of the government for "provocative moves" and renewed calls for elections and release of prisoners, and mosques again were the sites of frequent clashes with security forces. A percussion bomb explosion in a shopping mall on December 31 and an explosion caused by a small bomb in a restroom of the Meridian Hotel on January 17, 1996, during a conference of oil industry executives, triggered more arrests and clashes.[65] Shaikh al-Jamri and others were summoned to the Ministry of Interior regarding their speeches and public remarks. On January 23 the Ministry confirmed that al-Jamri, Abd al-Wahab Hussain, and others were under arrest.[66] A government official asserted, "There is proof,

---

[63] According to the U.S. embassy, more than 2,700 persons had been arrested in the first half of 1995, and some 2,100 had been released in the course of 1995 (U.S. Department of State, *Country Reports on Human Rights Practices for 1995* [Washington, D.C., 1996], p. 1129).

[64] See, for instance, the Agence France-Presse dispatch of January 12, 1996. As explained below, this case had been moved from the security court to the criminal court, and hence judicial appeal was possible.

[65] There were no injuries in either of these incidents. A number of Bahrain's five-star hotels are reportedly owned by the prime minister and his immediate family. Some attacks against such high-profile targets may have been related to this.

[66] The others were Hasan Mushaima, Ali Ahmad Howarah, Hasan Ali Muhammad Sultan, Ibrahim Adnan Nasir al-Alawi, Abd al-Ashur al-Satrawi, and Husain Ali Hasan al-Daihi. Several days later the government asserted it was holding 544 persons, including 174 from the latest clashes.

evidence, and documents supported by pictures which prove the group's involvement in the incidents and would be submitted to the legal authorities."[67]

As of May 1997, some sixteen months later, no charges had been filed against al-Jamri and his colleagues, and they have reportedly been allowed three brief visits by family members. In January 1996, there were signs that the government might declare martial law and employ the 8,000-man regular army—the Bahrain Defense Force, or BDF—alongside the roughly 11,000-strong Public Security Force.[68] To date, however, combating the internal unrest has

---

[67] Reuter, January 23, 1996.

[68] The BDF is an all-recruit force comprising Bahraini citizens only. In practice, only Sunnis are recruited, and the government has reportedly been recruiting Sunni Arabs from neighboring countries, particularly from among poor Sunni tribes in Syria, and granting them Bahraini citizenship in order to comply with this requirement. The Public Security Force, by contrast, is composed mainly of Pakistani and Baluchi recruits, a fact which, together with the role of Ian Henderson as head of security and the presence of other British advisors, accounts for the common opposition charge that they are a "mercenary" force.

A BDF statement on January 20, 1996, said, "The BDF is ready and prepared to perform its security role in the service of the homeland by taking the necessary military measures and provisions to settle the situation once and for all and put an end to all activities that harm security...." (Reuter, January 21, 1996). Many Bahraini observers attributed this verbal intervention to a long-standing rivalry between, on the one hand, Shaikh Hamad bin Isa Al Khalifa, the amir's son, crown prince, deputy prime minister, and commander of the BDF, and, on the other hand, Shaikh Khalifa bin Salman Al Khalifa, the amir's brother and, as prime minister, in charge of the paramilitary and police forces of the Interior Ministry. On December 9, 1996, when the prime minister was abroad and the crown prince assumed the acting prime ministership, BDF units were deployed in the capital and elsewhere in the country before being abruptly withdrawn in mid-afternoon (BFM, *Voice of Bahrain*, January 1996, p. 2).

The purported rivalry between the prime minister and the crown prince seemed to resurface again in January 1997 when, while the prime minister was on an extended trip abroad, the crown prince announced the creation of a "National Guard" which, unlike the BDF, could be employed against local unrest without a formal declaration of martial law ("Bahrain to form national guard to boost security," Reuter, December 24, 1996). It was unclear, as of this writing, whether the National Guard was being formed from designated units of the BDF or from recruits from Sunni tribes in Syria, Yemen and other countries in the region.

The manpower figures are from Cordesman, p. 108.

largely remained the task of the foreign-staffed security forces working under the Ministry of Interior and Director of Public Security Henderson.[69]

In the months that followed there were further bombings involving small, home-made devices, including a February 11 blast at the Diplomat Hotel that injured three people, a bombing of the car of the chief editor of *Al-Ayam,* a pro-government daily, in which no one was injured, and a blast at a branch of the National Bank that injured two persons and killed one, allegedly the perpetrator of the attack. In early March, a restaurant in Sitra frequented by Bangladeshi workers was firebombed and seven workers killed, bringing the number of fatalities since the unrest began in December 1994 to twenty-four, including three police and several confirmed cases of deaths in detention, reportedly as a result of torture and severe beatings.[70]

The government had been making liberal use of the security court to try hundreds of persons arrested in connection with the unrest. In the case of Isa Qambar, however, a twenty-nine-year-old accused of killing a policeman in March 1995, lawyers successfully petitioned the High Court of Appeal to rule, in May

---

[69] The U.S. Department of State *Country Reports on Human Rights Practices for 1996* chapter on Bahrain reports, "On May 3, Fadhil Abbas Marhoun of the village of Karzakkan was fatally shot by a patrolling BDF unit" (p. 1233). According to Cordesman, "Reports [uncited] that troops were used are false. Some of these reports may stem from the deployment of Bahraini armed forces on routine exercises" (p. 391, n. 80).

[70] The government made numerous arrests following the Sitra firebombing, and on July 1, 1996, the State Security Court sentenced three Bahrainis to death for the attack, despite numerous questions about their culpability and the fairness of the trial (see "Amnesty International USA and Human Rights Watch Call on the Government of Bahrain to Halt Impending Executions Following Severely Flawed Trial," October 30, 1996).

The death toll is from Reuter, March 20, 1996. With regard to deaths in detention, Amnesty International cites the case of Hussain Qambar, who had been detained in the wave of arrests in the second week of December and whose body was returned to his family on January 4, 1995, allegedly bearing traces of torture, including extracted fingernails. In another case, also cited in the U.S. Department of State *Country Reports on Human Rights Practices for 1995,* Sa`id Abd al-Rasul al-Iskafi, sixteen years old, died ten days after being summoned for interrogation. After examining photos of al-Iskafi's body, a forensic pathologist concluded that "the deceased has been subjected to ill-treatment of a sustained and very painful nature" (Amnesty International, *Bahrain: a Human Rights Crisis* [AI Index: MDE 11/16/95], September 1995). The U.S. Department of State *Country Reports on Human Rights Practices for 1996* refers to the death in detention of Sayyid Ali Amin, nineteen years old, on August 15, 1996. Regarding a formal complaint by Sa`id al-Iskafi's father to the deputy minister of interior, see below, note 118.

1995, that, as the security court, it did not have jurisdiction, and that the case should be tried in a criminal court. Qambar was convicted in criminal court, and his death sentence was subsequently upheld on appeal.[71] The government, however, was evidently concerned that this might set an unwelcome precedent and compel it to prosecute other destruction of property and bodily harm cases in the criminal court, with its higher standards of evidence and more substantial adversarial procedure.[72] On March 19, 1996, the government by decree transferred jurisdiction over some fourteen additional articles of the penal code from the criminal courts to the State Security Court.[73] The additional offenses that can now be prosecuted in the security court include arson and use of fires or explosives (Articles 277 - 281), and assaults or threats "against a civil servant or officer entrusted with a public service" (Article 220), or "against another in any manner, even though without having the intent of killing the victim, if the assault leads to death of the victim" (Article 336). Also in early 1996 the government quietly expanded the security court from one chamber to three chambers in order to cope with the increased number of arrests (see below). Over the following ten months, more than 180 persons were convicted under the state security process, compared with one estimate of fewer than fifty in 1995.[74] This period also saw increased detention of women and children.[75]

------

[71] Qambar was executed on March 26, 1996.

[72] The due process shortcomings of the security court are discussed in the next section. Bahrain's Ministry of Interior, in an introduction to a compilation of security laws and decrees dated November 1992 (Ref: LA/4/9), notes that, "It is basic to understanding the role of the judiciary that Bahrain criminal jurisprudence is inquisitorial rather than adversarial" (p. 2).

[73] Amiri Decree 10/1996, issued on March 19, 1996, and published in Official Gazette no. 2208, March 20, 1996.

[74] The 1996 figure is reported in "Bahrain Jails 11 for Arson Attacks," Reuter, January 19, 1997. The number for 1995 is from the U.S. Department of State *Country Reports on Human Rights Practices for 1996,* which says that "over 117 Security Court convictions were publicly acknowledged by the Government" for 1996. Bahraini defense lawyers told Human Rights Watch that the State Department figure for 1995 is certainly too low.

[75] See Amnesty International, *Bahrain: Women and Children Subject to Increasing Abuse* (AI Index: MDE11/18/96), July 1996.

In June 1995, the government announced changes in some cabinet positions. Key portfolios—prime minister, deputy prime minister, foreign affairs, defense, interior, justice and Islamic Affairs— remained unchanged in Al Khalifa hands. The appointment of Abd al-Nabi Shu`ala, a Shi`a businessman, as minister of labor and social affairs was hailed by some Western diplomats as a sign that the government was intent on addressing the unemployment and social welfare issues that were contributing to the unrest.[76] Bahraini critics, on the other hand, pointed to the replacement of Ali Fakhro, a reformist technocrat, as minister of education by General Abd al-Aziz al-Fadhil, formerly in charge of training for the BDF, as indicating that increased repression rather than liberal reform was behind the changes. Al-Fadhil quickly replaced Dr. Ibrahim al-Hashimi as president of the university with Colonel Muhammad Jasim al-Ghatam, a former BDF officer. Faculty members and respected Bahraini Shi`a professionals interviewed by Human Rights Watch have confirmed charges by opposition groups of increased discrimination against Shi`a applicants to the university and the dismissal of many Shi`a from senior positions.[77]

---

[76] Human Rights Watch interviews with British Foreign Office and U.S. State Department officials, London and Washington, March 1996.

[77] This is also reported in the Bahrain chapter of the U.S. Department of State's *Country Reports 1996*, section 2.a. In an undated memorandum to the secretary-general of UNESCO, the Committee for the Defense of Human Rights in Bahrain charged that al-Hashimi and other university officials were dismissed or transferred because they "refused to cooperate with the SIS and the security forces." "The office of Dr. al-Hashimi was searched, dossiers of wanted students were confiscated, and staff were arrested and interrogated." In his first meeting with university staff, the memorandum asserts, Colonel al-Ghatam stated, "The time of laxity has passed and the time of firmness has commenced." One faculty member told Human Rights Watch that al-Hashimi was replaced simply because he had been part of the former administration. According to this person, following the outbreak of the uprising in December 1994 security officials began to play an intrusive role in the hiring and dismissal of university faculty and staff and the admission of students, and that this influence has become even more direct and pervasive with former military officers formally in charge.

The Committee on Academic Freedom in the Middle East and North Africa, of the Middle East Studies Association of North America, wrote a public letter to Amir Isa on March 18, 1997, asserting that at least sixteen university students—all Shi`a males in advanced degree programs—had been dismissed since September 1996. The committee's letter characterized the university administration as one that had been "'cleansed' to implement entirely non-academic criteria."

Col. al-Ghatam asserted recently that university admissions selection was made

The problem of discrimination against Shi`a appears to be worsening. One Bahraini Shi`a told Human Rights Watch that he and a coworker had been dismissed from their jobs at an airlines sales office, located at the main airport, after their airport access passes were confiscated in August 1995. When the office manager contacted the authorities to look into the problem, he was reportedly told that "we don't want these kind of people working at the airport."[78] Human Rights Watch has also received numerous unconfirmed reports of new hiring and firing policies designed to reduce the number of Shi`a in ministries and state companies formerly considered to be Shi`a employment redoubts, such as the Ministry of Electricity and Public Works and BATELCO, the state telecommunications company.[79]

In early June 1996, the government announced that it had uncovered an Iranian-sponsored network which it called the "military wing of Hizb Allah

---

through an "advanced computer program" which was "subject to criteria and standards in the light of labor market requirements, development plans and the university's maximum capacity in certain specialisations" (*Bahrain Analysis* [London], no. 4, March 1997).

[78] Human Rights Watch telephone interview, November 1996.

[79] Human Rights Watch interviews, Manama, June 1996. *The Guardian* (London) quotes a "senior foreign banker" as saying: "If Bahrain is to preserve its reputation as a financial and service centre in the Gulf, then the government must begin to forge a new national consensus and end the apartheid against the Shi'ites" ("Crackdown on Shi'ites hurts Bahrain trade," June 20, 1996).

Bahraini critics of the government also contend that Shi`a perspectives are not reflected in school textbooks or in the media. According to a prominent Shi`a merchant, "If you switch on the TV, there is not a single program that refers to us, our history, our folklore, our geography" ("The two worlds of Bahrain: Shiite majority wants its share of Sunni-ruled nation's prosperity," *Washington Post*, June 13, 1995). Bahrain is the only Arab country in the Gulf that allows Shi`a religious processions to commemorate Muharram, but in April 1996 the government announced that it had established by decree a Higher Islamic Affairs Council to vet the qualifications of all Muslim religious scholars and clerics, thus ending the relative autonomy of the Shi`a religious establishment compared with that of the Sunni (Reuter, April 25, 1996). The Bahrain Freedom Movement subsequently wrote that senior Shi`a scholars protested in writing to the amir, declaring the council "unacceptable" ("Bahrain News," April 26, 1996). It is not clear that the government has since taken any steps to implement this decree.

Bahrain" and which it held responsible for the unrest since December 1994.[80] On June 5, 1996, the authorities broadcast live on television the confessions of several of the alleged ringleaders.[81] The government claimed to have secured confessions from twenty-nine persons detained earlier, and within several days announced that the number detained in connection with the alleged plot had risen to fifty-six. The government also claimed that the confessions implicated Shaikh Abd al-Amir as sanctioning the plan, and named several prominent exile opposition activists as co-conspirators, including Mansur al-Jamri and Sa`id al-Shihabi, with the Bahrain Freedom Movement in London, and Shaikh Khalil Sultan in Beirut. On March 1, 1997, security court hearings began for fifty-nine of the accused in custody and for twenty-two in absentia.[82] On March 26, 1997, in the first rulings in the case, a security court sentenced Ali al-Mutqawi to fifteen years, Jasim al-Khayyat to

---

[80] No known Bahraini opposition group goes by the name of "Hizb Allah" (Party of God), and no communications or publications have appeared under this name. It is a term used exclusively by the government to refer to the spectrum of Shi`a opposition forces, and in particular the Bahrain Islamic Freedom Movement. Ambassador Abdul Ghaffar, in his letter to Human Rights Watch, asserts that Shaikh Abd al-Amir al-Jamri and the other seven community leaders detained for more than fifteen months "are leading members of the terrorist group Hizbollah-Bahrain, primarily responsible for the terrorist campaign of violence and destruction." While the possible existence of a Bahraini group of this name cannot be excluded, the government's effort to attribute the past several years of political unrest to its machinations has no credibility.

[81] "Officials said Bahrainis had been excited about the televised testimonies. 'It is the first time we have had such a thing in Bahrain,' one said." ("Bahrainis implicate Iran in TV 'coup' confession," *The Guardian*, June 6, 1996.) One of those televised and alleged to be a leader of the scheme was Ali al-Mutqawi, whom the Bahrain Freedom Movement had earlier reported to have disappeared while crossing from Saudi Arabia into Jordan (BFM, May 22, 1996).

[82] "Bahrain to try suspected Islamic militants," Agence France-Presse, February 28, 1997. On March 17, 1997, Amnesty International issued a public call to halt the trials, which it said were "grossly unfair at all stages" (AI Index: MDE 11/03/97). A government official rejected the Amnesty appeal, asserting that "the defendants are enjoying a fair and just trial" and that "the defense lawyers were able to study the case and had access to the investigations, indictments and judicial confessions that the defendants made through a legal manner and without pressure or coercion." ("Bahrain rejects call to abandon trial of alleged coup plotters," Agence France-Presse, March 18, 1997.) According to the Bahrain Freedom Movement, based on information from lawyers, the defendants were being tried in batches of approximately seven each before the security court.

twelve years, and fourteen others to terms ranging from three to eight years. Eleven defendants were acquitted. Al-Mutqawi and al-Khayyat also were ordered to pay fines of more than $18,000 and $13,000, respectively. On March 29, twenty additional persons received sentences of up to seven years, and twelve were acquitted.[83]

In late 1996, the government announced that it had reached an agreement with the International Committee of the Red Cross allowing the ICRC access to Bahraini prisons and prisoners. An ICRC representative was in the country in late 1996 and early 1997, but, in keeping with ICRC policy, no findings have been announced or released.

---

[83] Agence France-Presse, "16 Iranian-backed militants jailed in Bahrain," March 26, 1997; Bahrain Freedom Movement, "More victims sentenced by Al-Khalifa judges," March 29, 1997. The Bahrain Human Rights Organization published a list of the names of all fifty-nine defendants, the disposition of their cases, and the length of sentence for each of those convicted (DK 9704062, April 6, 1997). One of Bahrain's pro-government dailies, *Al-Ayam,* wrote on March 27, 1997, that defense lawyers had expressed "satisfaction" with the verdicts and the conduct of the trials.

5. HUMAN RIGHTS VIOLATIONS

In terms of the number of persons affected, the human rights situation in Bahrain has deteriorated since the early 1990s, and particularly with the escalation of social and political unrest since late 1994. The pattern of violations and the categories of abuse, however, are consistent with policies and practices that extend back at least to the 1975 decision of the ruling family to abrogate those portions of the constitution relating to the National Assembly and elections. Many of these practices, furthermore, derive from the policies used by Great Britain prior to Bahrain's independence in 1971.

Human rights abuses in Bahrain can be divided into two basic categories. The first relates broadly to law enforcement and administration of justice issues. These encompass the behavior of police and security forces in arrest and detention; legal and institutional protections against arbitrary detention and against torture and cruel, inhuman or degrading treatment; access to legal counsel and to family visits; right to a swift and impartial trial; and the meaningful right to appeal a conviction to a higher judicial authority.[84] While any apprehended persons—citizen or foreign worker, Sunni or Shi`a—can be subjected to these abuses, the most serious and far-reaching violations affect persons accused of political and security-related offenses. In the decade after the abrogation of the constitution, and earlier under British rule, such abuses were mainly directed against persons connected with organized leftist and nationalist opposition groups, such as the Popular Front for the Liberation of Bahrain (PF) and the National Liberation Front (NLF). Since the Iranian revolution in 1979, and especially in the period since 1994, the victims have been mainly Shi`a Bahrainis, whether part of an organization such as the Islamic Front for the Liberation of Bahrain (IFLB) or as part of a larger, more diffuse politically disaffected community.

The second area of human rights violations relates to the broad denial of such civil and political rights as freedom of expression, freedom of association and assembly, and the right to participate in the conduct of public affairs, directly or

---

[84] These rights, generally recognized as constituting minimal guarantees of a fair trial, are enumerated in Articles 19 and 20 of the Bahraini constitution, and some are specified in Articles 8 through 11 of the Universal Declaration of Human Rights. Bahraini officials have asserted, "As a member of the United Nations, Bahrain fully recognizes its responsibility to uphold fundamental human rights and freedoms in accordance with the United Nations Charter and the Universal Declaration of Human Rights." See the letter by Dr. Muhammad Abdul Ghaffar, Bahrain's ambassador to the United States, in *Middle East Report* (October-December 1996), p. 48.

through freely chosen representatives.[85] All Bahrainis, Sunni and Shi`a alike, risk search and seizure, incarceration without charge or trial, and in some cases forced expulsion for speaking out publicly in a manner that the government regards as hostile or critical. Radio and television media is controlled by the state, and the print media exercises stringent self-censorship. Distribution or possession of unauthorized publications or leaflets constitutes grounds for detention. Bahrainis have been fired from their jobs and blacklisted from other employment for signing public petitions. Political parties and organizations, and independent trade unions, are forbidden. Public meetings and gatherings must be authorized by the authorities, and in practice they are not. Religious gatherings which, in the view of the government, raise political demands are routinely disrupted or prevented from occurring. Public advocacy of restoring Bahrain's partially elected National Assembly, in accordance with the constitution of 1973, is considered by the government to be a hostile act and grounds for detention without charge or trial under the State Security Measures Law of 1974 (see above). It is the government's systematic violation of these fundamental freedoms and political rights that has contributed to the conditions of confrontation in Bahrain today.

Violations of Due Process Rights
Bahrain's Courts and Legal System

Bahrain's legal system draws on a combination of customary tribal law (*urf*), three distinct schools of Islamic law (*shari`a*), and modern law, which was developed through 1971 largely by British colonial administrators and legal advisers and since then with the assistance of Egyptian advisers.[86] Shari`a courts have jurisdiction primarily over matters of personal status, such as marriage and inheritance. The civil court system, which is the concern of this report, comprises courts of first instance, with separate civil and criminal sections, and the High Court of Appeal.[87] The High Court of Appeal, in addition, sits as the special court established by decree pursuant to Article 185 of the 1976 Penal Code, with jurisdiction over persons prosecuted under the internal and external security

---

[85] These rights are enshrined in Articles 19, 20, and 21 of the Universal Declaration of Human Rights.

[86] The three Islamic schools of law are Maliki and Shafi`i, both recognized by Sunni Muslims, and the Ja`fari school recognized by Shi`a Muslims.

[87] See Hooglund, pp. 142-43.

provisions of the code.[88] The High Court of Appeal separately also sits as the venue for hearing complaints by persons detained without charge under the 1974 State Security Measures Law.[89]

Bahrain's constitution of 1973 characterizes the judiciary as a separate branch of the government. In practice, however, this independence is nominal. Abdallah bin Khalid Al Khalifa, the minister of justice and Islamic affairs, is responsible to the prime minister and brother of the amir, and is himself a member of the ruling family. The High Court of Appeal, which also sits as the State Security Court, includes two members of the ruling family, one of whom, Shaikh Abd al-Rahman bin Jabir Al Khalifa, is president of the court.[90] The office of public prosecutor, moreover, is attached to the Ministry of Interior, under Muhammad bin Khalifa Al Khalifa, a first cousin of the amir, and is thus institutionally linked to the state's security and intelligence services rather than to its judiciary. The Ministry of Interior is integrally involved in virtually every aspect of the judicial system and legal proceedings: as noted below, for example, sessions with the investigating judge take place in the Interior Ministry complex, and on those occasions when a medical specialist is assigned to review allegations of torture, that person is selected by the Interior Ministry and is generally the forensic medical officer of the Criminal Investigations Directorate.

---

[88] See above, note 22.

[89] Article 1 of the 1974 decree law states, "Anyone arrested under the provisions of the first paragraph may submit a complaint against the arrest order, after the expiry of three months from the date of its execution, to the Supreme Court of Appeal. The complaint is renewable at the end of every six months from the date of the decree rejecting the complaint." Article 2 specifies that the proceedings "shall always be held in camera." Article 3 states that, "The court, without observing the procedures stipulated in the Law of Criminal Procedures, may lay down the procedures to be followed by it...." (See above, note 18.) When sitting as the state security court, the court may elect to hold its proceedings *in camera*, and according to Bahraini defense lawyers, does so as a rule.

A security court chamber consists of three High Court of Appeal justices. In March 1996 the number of chambers was increased from one to three to accommodate the escalation of arrests and detentions.

[90] There are nine High Court of Appeal justices: the remainder are six Egyptians and one Sudanese ("Crackdown on Shi'ites hurts Bahrain trade," *The Guardian*, June 20, 1996, and Human Rights Watch interviews with Bahraini lawyers).

The constitution endorses a wide range of civil and political rights and procedural guarantees.[91] Some of these, such as guarantees against torture and forcible exile, are stated categorically, and actions of the authorities which violate these protections clearly violate Bahrain's constitution as well as international standards. Other guarantees, such as freedom of speech, are qualified by formulations such as "in accordance with the conditions and procedures specified by the law." Article 19 (b), for instance, states, "No person shall be arrested, detained, imprisoned [or] searched...except in accordance with the law and under the supervision of the judicial authorities." According to Article 20 (c), "An accused person shall be presumed innocent until proven guilty in a legal trial in which the necessary guarantees for the exercise of his right of defense in all stages of investigation and trial are ensured in accordance with the law."[92]

Most state constitutions have provisions that entrust to "the law" the regulation or expansion of basic constitutional protections. Laws that fail to do this are in violation of the constitution. Bahraini law, as embodied in the Penal Code of 1976 and other decrees discussed below, in many instances itself permits official behavior that contravenes the constitution and international standards. In Bahrain, moreover, the government has failed to comply with Article 103 of the constitution, which provides for a judicial body with the authority to review the constitutionality of laws and decrees.[93]

Among these laws are the State Security Measures Law of 1974, the state security court decree of 1976, and subsequent expansions and enlargements of the jurisdiction of these measures and this court. Consider, for instance, the State Security Measures Law, the decree which prompted the confrontation that led the ruling family in 1975 to dissolve the National Assembly and abrogate those articles

---

[91] Article 1, for instance, proclaims that "the system of government in Bahrain is democratic" and "citizens shall have the right to participate in the public affairs of the State, and enjoy political rights, beginning with the right to vote," though it also states that "the rule of Bahrain shall be hereditary." Articles 18, 19 and 20 cover a range of procedural guarantees, while Articles 22 through 29 provide for a wide range of civil and political rights.

[92] Unofficial translation of the constitution published in Arabic in the Official Gazette of the State of Bahrain, May 26, 1973, provided by the Bahrain Petroleum Company to the US Department of State, p. 9.

[93] Centre for the Independence of Judges and Lawyers, "Bahrain," in *Attacks on Justice: The Harassment and Persecution of Judges and Lawyers, January-December 1995* (Geneva), p. 53.

of the constitution pertaining to national elections (see above). This is a broadly written statute that authorizes search, seizure and up to three years of detention without charge or trial of any person against whom there is "serious evidence"—with no elaboration of what might comprise "serious evidence"—of "activities," "statements," or "contacts inside or outside the country,"

> which are of a nature considered to be in violation of the internal or external security of the country, the religious or national interests of the State, its social or economic system; or considered to be an act of sedition that affects or can possibly affect the existing relations between the people and Government, between the various institutions of the State, between the classes of people....

The government of Bahrain denies that its policies and practices are in violation of international human rights standards. An April 1995 official response to the Working Group on Arbitrary Detention of the U.N. Commission on Human Rights dismissed the Bahrain Human Rights Organization as "Hizbolla" and asserted:

> it is routine for such organizations to falsely allege torture, mistreatment, arbitrary arrest etc at the hands of the legitimate authorities whom they seek to discredit and to disseminate such falsehoods into the Human Rights Movement as a means of seeking international legitimacy for their patently unlawful cause...

> ...Human Rights are the cornerstone of Government Policies. Accordingly the Government has made every effort over the years to ensure that those policies are implemented throughout the Community and this is reflected in Bahrain's cultural traditions, strong constitution and extensive body of sophisticated Laws in which the fundamental rights and freedoms of the individual are codified and protected in accordance with the universally recognized Human Rights principles of the United Nations.

> ....In the face of any threat to those fundamental Human Rights and Freedoms the Government of Bahrain will in application of

the principles of Article 30 of the Universal Declaration of Human Rights and within the meaning of Article 5(1) of the International Covenant on Civil and Political Rights unhesitatingly act by whatever lawful means are at its disposal to protect the Bahrain Community, defend the Constitution, uphold the Rule of Law and ensure universal respect for Human Rights.[94]

Violations by Security Forces in the Process of Arrest

In response to the protracted unrest since December 1994, the government has detained thousands of persons and sentenced hundreds to jail terms and substantial fines. Some portion of those detained were rounded up during street confrontations with security forces, particularly in the early months of the uprising. More typically, however, security forces entered villages and neighborhoods, often in the aftermath of street clashes, seeking to arrest persons by name or en masse.[95]

These arrests generally took the form of house raids around or just after midnight. Hussain, a nineteen year old from Shahraqan, a town of about 200 families west of Manama, had been a student in Qom, Iran, and returned to Bahrain

---

[94] "Government Response Re: List of over 500 persons arrested in recent months; Ref: Communication no. G/SO 218/2 of 3 March 1995," April 22, 1995. Regarding the legality of the State Security Measures Law, the response asserts: "Never questioned by the courts in 20 years of practice." The response also asserts that "[t]here have been no arbitrary arrests" and that charges of incommunicado detention and torture are "standard propaganda." Article 5 (1) of the International Covenant on Civil and Political Rights. to which Bahrain is not a party but which the government cites above, states, "Nothing in the present covenant may be interpreted as implying for any State, group or person any right to engage in any activity or perform any act aimed at the destruction of any of the rights and freedoms recognized herein or at their limitation to a greater extent than is provided for in the present Covenant."

On this point, see also the response of the government to Human Rights Watch, which is appended to this report.

[95] According to a defense lawyer interviewed by Human Rights Watch, arrests during the first three or four months of the uprising featured separate arrest orders for individuals by name, each with a serial number. By the end of the first year, if not earlier, ministerial arrest orders no longer contained serial numbers, and single orders served to authorize multiple arrests (telephone interview, March 1997).

at the beginning of 1995. "I had been home about six months," he told Human Rights Watch.

> I was asleep at home. It was about 2:30 in the morning. We're not in the habit of locking our doors. I was wakened with a gun barrel in my back and pulled out of bed by my hair. There were about seven men in the room, and they punched and kicked me for about fifteen minutes. Two of them, including the officer, were Bahrainis. The soldiers were Pakistani. They ransacked the house. The Bahrainis were shouting that they came to find the paint for making graffiti and if they didn't find what they were looking for they would fuck my sisters. "We will break your Shi`a heads," they said. They sat me on the floor. Three of them had guns pointed at me, and they kicked me. Then I was handcuffed and brought downstairs, where there were about four vans and more soldiers. They hit me with gun butts as they took me to a car, and some were firing rubber bullets at the windows of houses close to ours. I asked if they had a warrant. "You're not worth a warrant," they said. I was taken to Qal'a [the Fort, referring to the central jail in Manama, attached to the Ministry of Interior], blindfolded, on the floor of the car, their feet on me..[96]

Akil, a seventeen year old from Barbar, told Human Rights Watch that the first time the security forces came to his house, in December 1994, he was not there:

> So I went to the police station myself. They had rounded up about forty people, looking for people responsible for killing a policeman. They only kept me one day.

------

[96] Human Rights Watch interview, Kuwait, May 1996. Bahrainis often used the term *jaysh* [army] to refer to the Public Security forces, most of whom are Pakistani. The army proper, the Bahrain Defense Force (BDF), is by law made up of Bahraini citizens (see above, note 68). The State Security Directorate and the Criminal Investigations Directorate, both presently headed by Ian Henderson, also employ Bahrainis as well as foreigners, and many of these Bahrainis are Shi`a.

The second time was in March 1995. We were leaving Shaikh
Abd al-Aziz school, which is near the interrogation headquarters.
I was released the morning of the second day. The headmaster
phoned twelve of us at home and told us not to come back to
school.

The next month, on April 6 [1995], the security forces broke into
my house about midnight and took me and about ten others from
the village. They beat me inside the house and threw me in a
jeep and took me to al-Khamis station. They left us standing all
night, and would come by every now and then to hit us. They
pulled our T-shirts up over our heads to serve as blindfolds.
Someone had been arrested that afternoon in Barbar and they
found a can of petrol. That seems to be what prompted our
roundup.[97]

Akil was arrested again in early January 1996 during a demonstration (see below),
and was subsequently picked up a fifth time in a dragnet. He fled Bahrain in early
March 1996.

The pattern of breaking into a suspect's home in the middle of the night
to make an arrest extends to cases of detained community leaders and persons
accused of instigating the unrest. In the case of Shaikh Ali Salman, for instance:

They came around 2 a.m. that Thursday morning, from the
Special Branch. Ten of them came in and searched my room,
and took books and cassettes. They found an early draft of the
petition. In the prison the next morning they handcuffed me to
a chair, blindfolded, facing a wall. They questioned me about the
petition and they accused me of instigating the marathon
incident.[98]

Shaikh Khalil Sultan told Human Rights Watch that the authorities came
for him around midnight, in early April 1995:

---

[97] Human Rights Watch interview, Kuwait, May 1996.

[98] Human Rights Watch interview, London, March 1996. Regarding the "marathon
incident," see above.

Three cars of soldiers and one with *mukhabarat* came for me. They searched the house for half an hour, then took me in the *mukhabarat* car, blindfolded, my hands tied tightly behind me with plastic rope that cut the skin badly, to the Ministry of Interior complex at Qal'a. They untied my hands and put me in a room. After half an hour, Adil Flaifil came in, very angry, and tells me they have arrested Shaikh Jamri and the others as well. He has a small gun in his hand, and he hit me with it several times on the head and in my face. That's all. I was kept in a waiting room there for a week, with many others, but we weren't allowed to talk with one another. Then they moved us to a part of the ASRY [Arab Ship Repair Yard], at the tip of Muharraq island, where the Ministry of Interior has some prison space, and brought us back to Qal'a regularly for interrogation about some vague and fantastic plots to "hit" the airport and other installations.[99]

One activist in the petition campaign was seized in April 1996 on suspicion of having arranged meetings for a BBC reporter with other critics of the government. "They came to my house about 11:30 at night," he told Human Rights Watch:

My wife woke me up. There were Colonel al-Wazzan and Colonel al-Uraifi standing in front of me. They'd surrounded [my town] and there were about twelve jeeps in front of my house. They searched the house. They took me with them back to my office and searched there too. They had closed off all the roads around the office.

It was similar when they arrested me in 1990. They attacked my home at about 4:30 in the morning. They took me to my office, a different one then, and searched that, too. I asked if they had a warrant. "You can see it in al-Qal'a," they said. I never did see one.[100]

---

[99] Human Rights Watch interview, Beirut, May 1996. For Shaikh Khalil's account of his role in prison negotiations, see above.

[100] Human Rights Watch interview, Manama, June 1996.

Human Rights Watch also spoke with a number of Bahraini lawyers active in defending political prisoners, who without exception confirmed this pattern of post-midnight searches and seizures. "The law on this point is fine," one lawyer told Human Rights Watch. "The Criminal Procedure Code of 1966 says warrants are needed for search and seizure, and police must be accompanied by two witnesses. But almost all the cases I see involve warrantless home raids in the very early hours of the morning."[101] According to another defense lawyer:

> Virtually all those who are arrested for political reasons—those who end up in the state security court or administrative detention or exile, whether it's for giving a sermon or distributing leaflets or throwing a Molotov or burning tires—the pattern is the same: they are taken in the early hours of the morning; their home is invaded by a large number of security people; the house is ransacked in the name of a "search"; often there is no chance to dress; and one cannot object or question or ask for a warrant or authorization without risking physical abuse.[102]

Torture and Abuse of Detainees, Denial of Access to Counsel, and Uncorroborated Confessions

Systematic beating as well as other forms of physical and psychological abuse of detainees are pervasive in Bahrain. According to Bahraini lawyers, virtually anyone caught up in Bahrain's police and security institutions is liable to mistreatment. Beatings are "common practice" and anyone "in the system" is vulnerable, one Bahraini lawyer told Human Rights Watch,

> whether you've been arrested for shoplifting or embezzlement or distributing [anti-government] leaflets or throwing a Molotov. Even court witnesses get beaten. Beatings are used to secure confessions, or information about other suspects. But there is also a sense that anyone in custody for whatever reason must deserve punishment, which ordinary police and security officials feel entitled to administer. The exception, of course, is if you

---

[101] Human Rights Watch interview, Manama, June 1996.

[102] Human Rights Watch interview, December 1996.

come from an important family with *wasta* [influence]. There is
an element of protection by virtue of social rank.[103]

The accounts of physical abuse provided by detainees to Human Rights
Watch were consistent with each other, with the patterns described by defense
lawyers, and with the findings of Amnesty International.[104] Seventeen-year-old
Akil told Human Rights Watch what happened after he was brought, with ten
others, to al-Khamis police station in April 1995 (see above):

> In the morning they took us individually to question us. They
> accused us of incitement, of raising money for detainees'
> families, of buying petrol. They took our fingerprints and
> photos. After that, for many days, they'd take us out of the cell
> in the middle of the night, around 2 a.m., to harass us. Some
> signed confessions but they still didn't get out. I wrote a paper
> saying I did not do anything but they kept me too. Then they
> sent us to the prison in Jaw. The police beat us with hoses there.
> We were there for six months, and during that time they took us
> back to Qal'a four times for interrogation. The interrogators
> were Khalid al-Wazzan, the one they called al-Sa'ati, and one
> called Adil. Four English police came one day to Jaw. They
> asked us how long we'd been there, and why. This was when the
> negotiations [with Shaikh al-Jamri] were going on, so we were
> released after that.
>
> After my next arrest, in January '96 in a demonstration, I was
> held at al-Na'im station for sixteen days, and we were beaten
> regularly. Those who beat us were Yusuf al-Arab, one they
> called Khalifa al-Shar, a Muhammad Mahmud, and a Lieutenant

---

[103] Human Rights Watch interview, December 1996.

[104] See, in particular, Amnesty International, *Bahrain: A Human Rights Crisis* (AI
Index: MDE 11/16/95), September 1995, pp. 31-38.

Abd al-Razzaq. I could read their names from under my blindfold.[105]

Hussain, a nineteen year old from Shahraqan, told Human Rights Watch what happened after he after he was brought to Qal'a early one morning:

> They took me upstairs to an office, I don't know whose. There they told me to stand on one leg and bray like a donkey. "What am I accused of?" I asked. "Get some manners," the officer said, and he hit me and left. Then someone came in wearing a *dishdasha* [traditional white shoulder-to-ankle garment worn by men in the Gulf]. I recognized him from photos I had seen: It was Adil Flaifil. He asked me if I was Hussain Shahraqani and I said yes. He had a piece of paper marked "confidential" on top, otherwise blank. He told me to sign it. I refused. They took me to a different room and trussed me up with a pole under my knees. There were four men, two in uniform. They kicked me and took turns hitting me with a hose. After half an hour of this they took me back to Adil Flaifil, who told me again to sign. I refused again. I went back and forth several times between the hanging and beating and the questioning. At one point he [Flaifil] asked for my hand. Two people held my hand, and he burned the back of my hand with his cigarette [displays light scars].

Hussain asserted that his tormentors on this occasion also used electricity to inflict pain. Adil Flaifil, he said, "attached some wires to a piece of metal he was holding against my hand. The shock knocked me to the floor."

"Then they took me into a corridor and put my cuffed hands over the top of a door," Hussain continued:

> so I was hanging with my toes just touching the ground. I fell down when they finally let me off the door, and they beat me with a hose again for what seemed like a long time. They said

---

[105] Human Rights Watch interview, Kuwait, May 1996. According to the Bahrain Freedom Movement bulletin of May 5, 1997, Khalil al-Sa'ati had been, in the words of an Interior Ministry statement to Reuter, "shot dead on Monday in a dispute with another military man."

they would charge me with bombings and planning attacks with bombs. Later they said I would only have to confess to incitement. I still refused. Finally they said I had to sign a statement that I would not do these things. That I did sign. They gave me one more beating, till my mouth bled, and then they let me go. I fled Bahrain the next week and stayed away for several months. I then went back to my family but I heard they were getting people in the village to say I was inciting people, so I left again.[106]

Hussain's testimony describing torture is consistent with testimony from prisoners who had been arrested prior to the current unrest in the country.[107] Hashim al-Musawi, who was arrested in 1988, he said, for non-violent anti-regime activity, told Human Rights Watch he had been tortured on six different occasions lasting several days each over a six-month period. The techniques he described included: being kept standing for days without access to a toilet; being dunked head first in a barrel of polluted water; having pins inserted underneath his fingernails and toenails which were then heated by a cigarette lighter; and being injected with substances that gave him chills and shakes and caused diarrhea.[108]

These testimonies are also consistent with those secured by Amnesty International, which in September 1995 reported that it had interviewed Bahraini torture victims inside and outside the country, and that the methods described were

---

[106] Human Rights Watch interview, Kuwait, May 1996.

[107] The Convention against Torture and Other Cruel, Inhuman or Degrading Treatment or Punishment, which Bahrain has not ratified, defines torture as "any act by which severe pain or suffering, whether physical or mental, is intentionally inflicted on a person for such purposes as obtaining from him or a third person information or a confession, punishing him or a third person for an act he or a third person has committed or is suspected of having committed, or intimidating or coercing him or a third person, or for any reason based on discrimination of any kind, when such pain and suffering is inflicted by or at the instigation of or with the consent or acquiescence of a public official or other person acting in an official capacity" (Article 1).

[108] Human Rights Watch interview, London, February 1997. Al-Musawi was subsequently sentenced to a five-year term by the security court. On his release, in August 1993, he was summarily expelled from the country (see below). He had also been detained without charge for several years in the early 1980s.

consistent with information the organization had received in earlier years.[109] In recent years the U.S. Department of State's annual *Country Reports* chapters on Bahrain have acknowledged that reports of torture were "credible," and have noted cases of deaths in detention attributable to torture and severe beating.[110] Several Bahraini lawyers told Human Rights Watch that, in their experience, mistreatment amounting to torture is commonplace. According to one lawyer, the severity of beatings and torture generally depends on the cooperativeness of the detainee in the process of securing a confession and follows a predictable sequence.[111] Once the authorities have gotten a confession, another lawyer told Human Rights Watch:

> the accused is left in his cell for several days. If he doesn't look too bad he is taken directly to the investigating judge, who looks at the statement—which the authorities have prepared and forced the defendant to sign—and asks, "Did you do X, Y, Z?" Or, "Did A,B,C happen like this?"[112] The defendant has already been instructed to answer yes, under threat of further abuse. Some complain of torture, and may even show the signs of torture

---

[109] Amnesty International, *Bahrain: A Human Rights Crisis*, pp. 31-38.

[110] Prior to 1994, by contrast, the U.S. State Department reports gave little credence to allegations of torture, although they acknowledged that practices of incommunicado detention and acceptance in court of uncorroborated confessions (see below) made it impossible to refute such charges. The report for 1993, for instance, said that "there were very few credible reports of torture," and that "Bahrain's small size and social structure would make it extremely difficult for the Government to conceal serious abuses if they were frequent or systematic" (p. 1157).

[111] Human Rights Watch interview, Manama, June 1996.

[112] According to Bahraini defense lawyers, sitting criminal and civil court judges are to be assigned to serve as investigating judges (*qadi al-tahqiq*) on a rotating basis by the Ministry of Justice, most probably in consultation with the Ministry of Interior. Excluding the most senior judges on the High Court of Appeal, approximately twelve judges are in this pool. In practice, according to all Bahraini defense lawyers who spoke with Human Rights Watch, the ministry relies on two judges, Sa'ad al-Shamlan and Abdallah Budair, for registering almost all confessions in criminal and security cases, with al-Shamlan being assigned to most of the security cases. According to the lawyers, this is because the government knows it can rely on al-Shamlan and Budair to accommodate the prosecution fully.

clearly, but the investigating judge dismisses or ignores such claims. If the defendant disagrees with the statement, however, or starts to qualify it, the investigating judge says, "Your man is not done yet." In other words, either amend the statement or get him to confess "accurately." This is when the torture gets severe, and moves from beatings to combinations of sleep, food and toilet facilities deprivation, being forced to lie face down while security forces walk over you with heavy boots, or being beaten while hung up by a pole behind the knees. Very few endure more than several hours of this. The last phase, for those who do hold out longer, is electric shock or pulling out toenails.[113]

Torture is categorically prohibited by Bahrain's constitution and penal code.[114] The government of Bahrain, in its response to Human Rights Watch, asserts that allegations of torture "are simply not true, and propagandist in nature," and that "there are internal procedures for the investigation of complaints against the police."[115] There are no known instances, however, where Bahraini authorities have conducted an investigation as a result of allegations of torture, or where anyone in a position of responsibility has been punished for inflicting torture.[116]

---

[113] Human Rights Watch interview, December 1996.

[114] Article 19(d) of the Constitution states, "No person shall be subjected to physical or mental torture, enticement or degrading treatment, and the law shall provide penalty for these acts. Any statement or confession shall be null and void if it is proved to have been made under duress or enticement or degrading treatment or threat thereof."

Article 208 of the 1976 Penal Code states, "A prison sentence shall be the penalty for every civil servant or officer entrusted with a public service who uses torture, force or threat, either personally or through a third party, against an accused person, witness or expert to force him to admit having committed a crime or give statements or information in respect thereof. The penalty shall be life imprisonment should the use of torture or force lead to death."

[115] Letter of Ambassador Muhammad Abdul Ghaffar, reproduced as an appendix to this report.

[116] One Bahraini lawyer told Human Rights Watch that disciplinary measures have most likely been taken against officials when torture has led to death in detention, but this person could cite no known instance of this happening (interview, December 1996).

The government further claims that "anyone so aggrieved has the right [of] recourse to the courts under the law. However, no-one has done so and no formal complaints have been made."[117] Bahraini defense lawyers told Human Rights Watch that they habitually raise the issue of physical abuse before the courts, and point out that the medical personnel who examine the defendants themselves work directly for the Ministry of Interior, as does the public prosecutor who would, in theory, file and prosecute complaints.[118]

Human Rights Watch also spoke with detainees who had not been subjected to torture or systematic beatings. Those caught up in street arrests, it seems, sometimes avoided this fate. "Haphazard arrests are more haphazardly mistreated," was how one lawyer put it.[119] Human Rights Watch also found that more prominent opponents of the government were less harshly treated. Ahmad al-Shamlan, a prominent lawyer and activist in the petition campaign who was arrested in February 1996, told Human Rights Watch that during one interrogation session Adil Flaifil shouted, "I have orders not to touch you, but I'll keep you here

---

[117] Letter of Ambassador Muhammad Abdul Ghaffar. Ian Henderson, the Scotsman who heads the Criminal Investigations and State Security Directorates, reportedly acknowledged recently that "vigorous interrogation" is common, but Henderson also insisted, "I've never lifted a finger against anyone, or asked officers to do so.... I don't do nine-tenths of what I'm accused of" (Neil Mackay, "No Blood on My Hands," *The Big Issue* [Edinburgh], December 28, 1996 - January 8, 1997).

[118] Interviews, Manama, June 1996. Human Rights Watch has a copy of a letter written by Abd al-Rasul Hasan al-Iskafi to the deputy minister of interior, dated July 12, 1995, requesting an investigation into the death in detention of his son, Sa`id. According to the letter, police raided the family home on the night of June 28, 1995, looking for Sa`id, who was not there at the time. The next morning his father instructed him to report to the nearest police station, which the sixteen year old did. "On July 8th," the letter continues, "we got a call from the ministry saying that our son's health had deteriorated and that we should go to the military hospital. We went to ask about him, but found him as a stiff corpse. We note he was in good health and had no ailments. When washing his body [for burial] we found evidence of brutal torture as well as sexual assault.... If he had committed an error, you would have the right to interrogate and discipline him according to that error, through the competent courts and according to procedures set forth in law.... I am full of hope that you will look into his case with compassion and will investigate the person who committed this ugly crime...." As far as Human Rights Watch has been able to determine, al-Iskafi received no response to his letter and no investigation ensued (see above, note 70).

[119] Human Rights Watch interview, November 1996.

three years," referring to the maximum period for detention without charge under the State Security Measures Law of 1974.[120]

Shaikh Ali Salman told Human Rights Watch that at one point his interrogators hit him with their fists and made him stand for prolonged periods. Otherwise he was not physically abused, he said, but the abuse of others was used to secure his confession:

> They brought two young men into the room, Muhammad and Ali. They were not in good shape, hardly able to stand. They asked them if I had told them to protest the marathon. They said no. They took them out and an hour later they brought Muhammad back, in much worse shape. This time he said, yes, I did instigate him. In the night they brought another man, Abd al-Ghani. First he refused to say I had told him to protest, and four hours later when they brought him back he said, yes, I had.

> They kept me in detention room number one. That night I could hear screams. I decided I should accept responsibility. At 11 the next morning I was taken to the investigating judge. They warned me not to change my mind in front of the judge.[121]

On the question of torture, Human Rights Watch also spoke with five practicing defense attorneys, whose testimony was consistent. "The biggest problem," one widely respected lawyer said:

> is the absence of transparency and accountability. Bahrain's judicial system is, on the whole, not bad, but not when the justices are sitting as the state security court. One-step litigation is inherently dangerous. Mistakes occur and go unchecked. There are no checks on the police. The public prosecutor, in the Ministry of Interior, decides who will be tried in the regular

---

[120] Human Rights Watch interview, Manama, June 1996. Shamlan had been arrested on a number of occasions dating back to 1965. In August 1981 he was arrested on returning from several years as a student in Moscow and detained for five years without charge or trial, including six months in solitary confinement.

[121] Human Rights Watch interview, London, March 1996.

court, who in the state security court, and who will simply be
detained without any charge at all.

In so-called security cases there is no access to legal counsel.
Nor are lawyers permitted at the next stage, when defendants are
brought before the investigating judge, who takes their
statements.

Nominally the investigating judge is a functionary of the
Ministry of Justice, but the "examination" takes place in the
Interior Ministry complex, which is also the main prison and
interrogation center. The strange thing is that nearly all the
security cases are heard by one man, Sa`ad al-Shamlan. And as
time went on the confessions all started to read the same, exactly
the same, as if they were using some kind of form-confession.[122]

Once a confession is finalized, another lawyer told Human Rights Watch:

the statement goes to a committee comprising Adil Flaifil,
Khalid al-Wazzan, and Abd al-Aziz Atiyatallah. This is not a
formal procedure, just what usually happens. They decide
whether the case will go to state security court or to the criminal
court after all, or whether to hold the persons without charge
under administrative detention [under provisions of the 1974
State Security Measures Law]. The papers then go to the public
prosecutor who gathers the needed statements or
documents—from the fire department, for instance, in cases of
arson—and assembles the file to present to court. This frequently
takes another five or six months, and sometimes as long as a
year. Then it goes to the Ministry of Justice to schedule a court
date. That's when the Ministry of Interior calls the family, tells
them to get a lawyer. This is usually the first official notification

---

[122] Human Rights Watch interview, Manama, June 1996.

of the exact charges against the defendant, though families usually manage to find out informally.[123]

Amiri Decree 7/1976 declared the High Court of Appeal, sitting as the so-called State Security Court, to be "the court competent to look into crimes provided for in Articles 112 to 184 of the Penal Code of 1976 as per Article 185 of the said Code." The decree stipulates that an accused person be represented by lawyer, and that the prosecutor should make available a case brief to the court and the defense "well in time, before the sitting of the court." The question of whether or not the trial should be open or *in camera* is left to the court's discretion, depending on "the supreme interest of the peace and security of the State." In practice, according to Bahraini lawyers, sessions of the security court are almost always closed to the public, including members of the defendant's family.[124] Uncorroborated confessions, secured in the absence of legal counsel, are sufficient for conviction in the cases it hears. The decree states in Article 3, paragraph 5:

> The confession of the accused, whether made against himself or against other co-accused, shall be weighed with care by the court and whether the said confession was made to the investigating judge or in court during trial or was made only in the course of the investigation by the public prosecutor or in the statement to the public prosecutor or the police.
>
> The court may act on this confession for its judgment.
>
> However, the provisions contained in this paragraph shall not apply to crimes punishable with death and the confession of the accused alone shall not avail [i.e., serve as the basis for

---

[123] Human Rights Watch interview, December 1996. According to the Bahrain Freedom Movement (June 8, 1997), in early June 1997 Abd al-Aziz bin Atiyatallah Al Khalifa was appointed governor of Manama, the capital.

[124] Occasionally, with high-profile trials, family members are allowed to attend the first session, when charges are read, but are barred from further sessions.

conviction] against such crimes unless it has been made in court
or before the investigating judge.[125]

Lastly, the court's verdict "shall be final and shall not, in any manner, be
challenged" (Article 7).[126] The Interior Ministry, in a document dated November
1992, explained the denial of a right to appeal conviction before the security court,
in contravention of international fair trial standards, in the following terms:

> Bringing such cases (from the investigatory/remand level) direct
> to the High Court of Appeal [sitting as the State Security Court]
> therefore serves the higher public interest by enabling matters
> concerning National Security to be dealt with promptly and
> authoritatively without raising public concern and wasting time
> by going through the sterile formalities of hearings in the
> intermediatory [sic] Courts.[127]

The initial State Security Court hearing is the first point at which the
accused gets to meet with a lawyer. The lawyer first sees the client's file a few days
in advance. "You meet your client in the large hall where the State Security Court
hearings take place in the old coast guard headquarters in Muharraq.," one lawyer
told Human Rights Watch:

> So you have maybe ten prisoners all talking to their lawyers in
> the same space in the twenty minutes before the hearing begins.
> The lawyer always advises the defendant to plead innocent, as a
> precautionary step to get a postponement of a week or so for a

---

[125] Ambassador Abdul Ghaffar asserts in his letter to Human Rights Watch that
"the [security] court is bound by the normal rules of evidence," and specifically the 1966
Code of Criminal Procedure, "which includes a provision that no confession made to a
policeman shall be admitted in evidence. Accordingly, for a confession to be admissible to
the court there must be corroboration." This is apparently true for ordinary criminal court
procedure in Bahrain. As the text of the security court law and the practice of the authorities
make clear, the ambassador is mistaken in his contention that it applies to state security court
procedures as well.

[126] Amiri Decree No. 7/1976 Concerning the Formation and Procedures with
Respect to Court Provided for in Article 185 of the Penal Code, issued on June 2, 1976.

[127] Introduction to a compilation of security laws and decrees (Ref: LA/4/9), p. 9.

second hearing, to have time to prepare a case, seek witnesses, arrange for documents. And usually you are representing more than one defendant at any given hearing. There is no formal rule that prevents you from meeting with your client between hearings, but in practice the security services never quite manage to allow it to happen.[128]

The structure and procedure of the state security court, in particular the admissibility and sufficiency for conviction of confessions secured in the absence of legal counsel and in the course of extended detention, effectively sanctions torture and abuse. Because the first court hearing may be as long as a year or more after the time of arrest, moreover, and never less than five or six months afterwards, physical marks of abuse have often disappeared. "We don't see our clients for a year, on average," one defense lawyer told Human Rights Watch. "By that time, when we go to the judge, there may be no evidence of abuse."[129] In entering pleas of innocence, lawyers do regularly contend that the confession had been secured under duress, in violation of the constitution. Lawyers told Human Rights Watch that in some cases the justices do order a medical examination; as noted above, this is generally the forensic medical officer of the Criminal Investigations Directorate, an employee of the Ministry of Interior. Even in cases where a defendant still shows unmistakable signs of torture, lawyers say, the justices proceed with conviction and sentencing. One lawyer familiar with the case of the young men charged and convicted in the firebomb attack that killed seven Bangladeshi workers (see above) told Human Rights Watch that one of the defendants had been tortured by having his toenails pulled out. "I saw the toenails myself," this lawyer said:

and his lawyer tried to present them to the judge but he found it all too disgusting and refused to look. He finally did order a medical exam. The Ministry of Interior arranged for a doctor, supposedly independent, from the Ministry of Health to do the exam. The doctor's statement concluded that there were "no signs" of torture, although it contained several discrepancies.[130]

---

[128] Human Rights Watch interview, December 1996.

[129] Human Rights Watch interview, Manama, June 1996.

[130] Human Rights Watch interview, December 1996.

A defense lawyer familiar with the Sitra case told Human Rights Watch that in this incident more than one group of detainees had confessed. "They have submitted to trial the group where they think they have the best evidence," he said, "but they do have more than one set of confessions."[131]

In response to the government's denial that torture and abuse occur on any scale, Bahraini defense lawyers point to the great number of identical accounts by detainees and the refusal of authorities to allow lawyers to be present during interrogation. "In my twenty years of experience, " one lawyer said, "torture is quite routine."[132] In the view of another lawyer:

> the refusal of the authorities to allow us to be present at the investigation stage, or even at the recording or examination stage, suggests that it is a serious problem. One of my clients, when I asked why he confessed and was now denying the charges, told me, "Even one of these judges could be forced to say he was Hizb Allah, the things they do to you."[133]

Arbitrary Detention

Bahraini authorities can detain persons for extended periods without charge or trial in two different ways. As discussed above, under the terms of the State Security Measures Law of 1974, the minister of interior may detain someone for up to three years, with a right to appeal the detention order after three months and at six-month intervals thereafter. Under Article 8 of that law, moreover, Article 79 of the criminal procedure code of 1966 was amended to allow an investigating judge to detain a suspect for an unlimited period, with the right of appeal after one month and on a monthly basis thereafter. The government does not provide information regarding the number of persons who have been or are being detained without charge under these distinct provisions of the State Security Measures Law. The decision to detain a person without charge under the terms of this law, as noted in the previous section, rests with the public prosecutor, under the Ministry of the Interior. Bahraini defense lawyers told Human Rights Watch that these provisions are used extensively by the government to incarcerate persons detained by the

---

[131] Human Rights Watch interview, Manama, June 1996.

[132] Human Rights Watch interview, Manama, June 1996.

[133] Human Rights Watch interview, Manama, June 1996.

security forces.[134] While such detentions can be appealed, these appeal proceedings must be held in secret and do not follow criminal court procedures.[135]

One indication of the extent of arbitrary detention is the apparent discrepancy between the large number of persons detained in 1996, the number of convictions, and the number remaining in detention.[136] The number of those detained without charge includes some of Bahrain's most prominent political prisoners. Shaikh Abd al-Amir al-Jamri, an elected member of the National Assembly and a prominent *shari`a* court jurist, and Abd al-Wahab Hussain, a teacher and leading community activist, together with half-a-dozen other Shi`a religious and community leaders, were held without charge for six months in 1995, from late March until late September. Al-Jamri, Hussain and six others were detained again on January 22, 1996. The next day, a Ministry of Interior official, referring to renewed demonstrations and attacks on property, told Reuter that "[t]here is proof, evidence and documents supported by pictures which prove the group's involvement in the incidents and would be submitted to the legal authorities" and that the eight had "incited crimes of fires and sabotage, broadcast statements, news and incorrect rumors inside and outside...which disturbs security and damages national interests using mosques and sermons and holding illegal gatherings."[137] As of May 1997, some sixteen months later, none have been formally charged with any offense, or been permitted access to legal counsel, and no evidence as to their responsibility for violent acts or the incitement of others to commit violent acts has been forthcoming. According to members of his family, Al-Jamri was kept in solitary confinement for more than nine months, and he and the other detained leaders have been allowed brief family visits only on three occasions.

---

[134] Human Rights Watch interviews, May 1997.

[135] See above, note 89.

[136] Ambassador Abdul Ghaffar, in his letter to Human Rights Watch, asserts that "all those arrested in connection with the recent unrest are ... either convicted by the independent courts or released." The U.S. State Department estimates that more than 3,000 persons were detained in 1996 (including some detained more than once), 117 were convicted by the state security court, and some 1,500 were in detention at year's end (U.S. Department of State, *Country Reports on Human Rights Practices for 1996*, p. 1234).

[137] Reuter, January 23, 1996.

As in the case of persons held without charge, the government of Bahrain does not provide information regarding the number of persons arrested or their disposition, including the number referred to the security court or the criminal court.[138] Many names of persons arrested and convicted are reported by the Bahrain Freedom Movement, based in London, and by the Bahrain Human Rights Organization in Copenhagen and the Committee for the Defense of Human Rights in Bahrain in Damascus. This information is provided by lawyers in Bahrain but, because of government restrictions and harassment, access to such information is limited. "Many convictions are not reported," one lawyer told Human Rights Watch. "The cases reported by the BFM represent a considerable part of the total, but certainly not all."[139] One measure of the extended use of the security court was its expansion in early 1996 from one court to three.

Violations of Political Rights
Bahrain's constitution guarantees freedom of speech (Article 23), the press (Article 24), communication (Article 26), association, including the right to form trade unions on a national basis (Article 27), and assembly (Article 28). In many cases, however, the 1976 Penal Code effectively nullifies those rights, particularly in the following articles:

•   Article 134A calls for imprisonment and a fine for "any citizen who has attended abroad in whatever capacity and without authorization from the Government, any conference, public meeting or seminar, or has participated in any manner whatsoever in the deliberations thereof with the intent of discussing political, social or economic conditions in the State of Bahrain or in any other state so as to weaken financial confidence in the State of Bahrain or undermine its prestige or standing or to worsen political relations between Bahrain and these countries."[140]

•   Article 163 more broadly penalizes "any person who establishes, sets up, organizes or runs in the State of Bahrain without a license issued by the

---

[138] As noted above (note 136), the U.S. embassy in Manama estimated that "over 3,000 people" had been held in detention in 1996, and that "[a]t year's end, as many as 1,500 detainees still remained in detention."

[139] Human Rights Watch interview, February 1997.

[140] This article was added to the penal code by decree in March 1982.

Government, international societies, organizations or institutions of any kind whatsoever or branches thereof," or "any person who joins the aforesaid societies, organizations and institutions," including any citizen who "join[s] or participate[s] in any manner without a Government license in any of the aforesaid organizations which are based outside the country."

- Article 164 authorizes the closure and dissolution of "aforesaid societies, organizations and institutions."

- Article 165 authorizes an unspecified prison sentence for "any person who expressly incites others to develop hatred or hostility toward the system of government."[141]

- Article 168 penalizes "any person who deliberately disseminates false reports, statements or malicious rumors, or produces any publicity seeking to damage public security, terrorize the population or cause damage to the public interest," and penalizes possession of "any publication or leaflet" containing such material or possession of any device intended for the reproduction or dissemination of such material.[142]

- Article 169 penalizes publication of "untrue reports" that "undermine the public peace or cause damage to the country's supreme interest or to the State's creditworthiness."

- Article 178 proscribes any assembly of five or more persons "aimed at undermining public security, even though for the realization of a legitimate objective."

- Article 222 penalizes "any person who offends with the use of signs, saying, writing or by any other method a civil servant or officer entrusted with a public service."

All of these offenses except the last (Article 222) come under the automatic jurisdiction of the State Security Court (see above). The exceedingly

---

[141] Article 165 is among those revised by decree in 1982.

[142] Article 168 is also among those revised by decree in 1982.

broad language of these articles is compounded further by Articles 166 and 167 of the penal code, which are also among those revised for retroactive application in 1982 and which specify imprisonment "for any person who resorts to violence, intimidation *or any other illegal method*" to pressure government officials (emphasis added).[143]

The broad effect of these laws by decree, and their application by the authorities, is that in Bahrain there are no legal political parties or independent trade unions. Political gatherings are proscribed. Telephone communications are monitored, and for a period in early 1996 the government prohibited the placing of international calls from public telephones.[144] Several persons in Bahrain told Human Rights Watch that government offices have instituted strict controls on the use of photocopy and fax machines.[145] Bahrainis interviewed for this report, including prominent businessmen, professionals, and former officials, insisted that their names not be cited for fear of arrest, dismissal or pressures or reprisals against their employers or businesses.[146]

Freedom of Association

Bahrain's constitution (Article 27) guarantees the "freedom to form associations and trade unions on a national basis and for lawful objectives and by peaceful means." In practice, authorized and licensed civic organizations, such as cultural and sports clubs, are closely monitored and effectively prevented from conducting discussions that deal with internal Bahraini political matters. Legislative decree 21/1989 stipulates that societies and clubs "shall not engage in politics" (Articles 18 and 63), and outlaws any society established for an illegal or immoral purpose "or should the object thereof prejudice the well-being of the state, form of

---

[143] Also among those articles revised by decree in 1982, Article 166 specifies life imprisonment when such pressure is directed against the amir or the prime minister.

[144] "'Political' Execution Stokes Unrest in Bahrain," *The Times* (London), March 27, 1996; "Bahrain: Prince's Police Strike Terror into Opposition," *The Independent* (London), February 19, 1996.

[145] Human Rights Watch interviews, Manama, June 1996.

[146] Bahrainis and foreign residents in Bahrain have told Human Rights Watch that all employers, in the private as well as the public sectors, must submit the names of prospective employees to the Ministry of Interior for a "security clearance."

government or its social system" (Article 3).[147] The law allows the government to reject the registration of a society if it deems its services or purposes unnecessary or "not compatible with the security of the state [or] its interests" and can effect such a rejection merely by not responding favorably to an application or to a complaint (Article 11). Article 33 requires organizers of general meetings to provide the agenda and fifteen days prior notification, and permits the government to "designate the person it deems fit for attending the said meeting," and Article 38 requires that minutes and resolutions be provided to the government within fifteen days of the meeting. Article 80 empowers the government "to control [private] organizations and to amend their constitutions so as to ensure the realization of the objects for which they are established." Article 13 effectively bans independent trade unions by stipulating that all labor-related activities be undertaken by the official General Committee of Bahraini Workers and Joint Labor-Management Committees.[148]

One of the oldest and most prominent social organizations is the Uruba Club, a self-styled cultural club founded in the 1930s, which played a critical role in the era of British rule as a site for political debate and networking. The Uruba Club now has upwards of 500 members, chiefly businessmen and professionals. Physically and in terms of activities it resembles a traditional British or American "gentleman's club." Some members met with Human Rights Watch in June 1996 to describe the club's relationship with the government and the constraints on its activities.

The Uruba Club comes under the authority of the General Organization for Youth and Sports, headed by Shaikh Isa bin Rashid Al Khalifa, and is required

---

[147] The decree's formal title is "With regard to promulgating the law of social and cultural societies and clubs, associations carrying on youth and sports activities and private organizations."

[148] There are sixteen Joint Committees based in larger state-owned and private firms comprising equal numbers of appointed management and elected labor representatives. The General Committee comprises eleven members elected for two-year terms by the labor members of the Joint Committees. Expatriate workers, though they are underrepresented, do participate in the Joint Committees. According to the U.S. Department of State *Country Reports on Human Rights Practices for 1996*, the 1995 General Committee elections "were by secret ballot and appeared to be free." As noted in the State Deparment report, the labor law "is silent on the right to strike," and "actions perceived to be deterimental to the 'existing relationship' between employers and employees or to the economic health of the State are forbidden by the 1974 [State] Security [Measures] Law."

to get permission for any event open to the public.[149] "We tried to have a public event last February [1996] on the theme of freedom of the press and condemning violence," one member said. "They [the General Organization] said OK on the phone, but then they asked for a list of invitees and told us we had to get permission from the Interior Ministry. We wrote for that but never got a reply." An effort around the same time to devote a monthly internal meeting to the topic of "shura and democracy" was similarly frustrated. "Internal meetings don't require permission," Human Rights Watch was told, but:

> because we were proposing to invite a Sunni and a Shi`a shaikh
> as outside speakers, we had to request permisssion. We called
> Khalid al-Hamad, a director in the General Organization, well-
> disposed but a bureaucrat. He called back to say we couldn't do
> it. Forbidden. Too sensitive a concept. We received an official
> letter a few days later reprimanding us for scheduling an
> "unauthorized meeting." This violated the statute of the clubs, it
> said, and we'd better not repeat this mistake. All the topics for
> our internal meetings are now very tame, very carefully selected.
> The circle we cannot enter is local politics. We can't discuss
> today's headlines in any kind of a questioning way. We had a
> meeting on the question of unemployment, and felt we could
> only do that by inviting the minister of labor to speak.[150]

Another club member told Human Rights Watch about an incident in 1995, when Shaikh Isa bin Rashid asked each club to sign a "loyalty pledge" to the amir:

> [He asked] even the [Shi`a] clubs in Diraz and Sanabis, just to
> humiliate them. They were all called to send a representative to
> the Amiri Court. Uruba refused to sign, but then the minister of
> information called our president and put very heavy pressure on
> him to sign. So we did. Later we heard that Shaikh Isa bin

---

[149] According to the law, the Ministry of Labor and Social Affairs is the "Concerned Administrative Authority" for "societies in general" and the General Organization for Youth and Sports is the authority for youth and sports clubs "and the other clubs not subject to the supervision of the Ministry of Labor and Social Affairs."

[150] Human Rights Watch interview, Manama, June 1996.

Rashid had commented to someone, "You see, they came like dogs."[151]

One professional association, the Bahrain Bar Association, has been allowed some leeway by the authorities to deal with political matters, having "successfully argued that a lawyer's professional duties may require certain political actions, such as interpreting legislation or participating in a politically sensitive trial."[152] According to one account, the Bar Association has successfully resisted government efforts to compel it to join other organizations in "congratulating" the government for mass arrests of alleged conspirators, on the grounds that as lawyers many of them would be called upon to defend those arrested.[153] At the same time, the Bar Association has tended to avoid dealing with issues such as human rights which the government regards as politically objectionable.

Freedom of Speech
Freedom of speech and the right to express political opinions are also severely circumscribed in Bahrain. In December 1991, Shaikh Abd al-Latif al-Mahmud, a professor of Islamic Studies at Bahrain University and a theologian prominent in Sunni Islamist circles, attended a seminar in Kuwait. In his presentation, Shaikh Abd al-Latif reportedly argued in favor of the institutionalization of elected legislative assemblies in the Gulf countries as checks on the powers of the ruling families, and advocated clearer separation between those countries' public finances and the private purses of the ruling families. When he returned to Manama on December 14, he was arrested, interrogated, and charged before the State Security Court for "abusing the regime" and "provoking popular hostility" to the government. Although he was released on bail on December 28, and in May 1992 all charges were dismissed by the court, Shaikh Abd al-Latif was dismissed from his university position and was not permitted to resume teaching until the fall of 1996.

---

[151] Human Rights Watch interview, Manama, June 1996.

[152] U.S. Department of State, *Country Reports on Human Rights Practices for 1996*, p. 1236.

[153] See, for example, Lawyers Committee for Human Rights, "The Legal Profession in the State of Bahrain," February 1992, p. 5.

A number of Shi`a clerics have been detained for varying lengths of time as a result of speeches or public discussions that were critical of the government. Shaikh Abd al-Amir al-Jamri, for instance, at the time of his re-arrest in January 1996, was accused by Interior Ministry spokespersons in the media of "play[ing] a major role in inciting crimes of riots and sabotage and escalating them."[154] But the government has produced no evidence that Shaikh al-Jamri or the seven other community leaders arrested with him have participated in or advocated violent or illegal acts. What is known about their activities indicates that they have been incarcerated for publicly advocating that Bahrain's National Assembly be reinstated, national elections held, and political prisoners freed.[155] Human Rights Watch has asked representatives of the government of Bahrain and persons covering Bahrain for the U.S. Department of State to make available any remarks by Shaikh al-Jamri that would support the contention of the government of Bahrain, but none have been made available.

Human Rights Watch is not aware of any instance where the Bahraini authorities have detained a person solely for signing one of the several petitions since 1992 calling for elections and restoration of the parliament. Persons have been detained, however, for promoting and disseminating the petitions, or for making the contents available to or discussing the petition campaign with international media. Ahmad al-Shamlan, a lawyer and long-time political activist who was prominently involved in the Popular Petition Committee, was arrested on February 7, 1996, immediately after a statement of the committee had been provided to Agence France-Presse:

> They came to my house at 4 a.m. They had a warrant, and they searched the house. All they found was a fax from Mansur al-Jamri asking about

---

[154] Reuter, January 23, 1996.

[155] On September 26, 1995, following his release after nearly six months in prison without charge, Shaikh al-Jamri reiterated, "The parliament comes at the top of our demands." On January 10, 1996, less than two weeks before he was re-arrested, Shaikh al-Jamri spoke to thousands of persons attending Sadiq mosque, one of Bahrain's largest, in the town of Diraz, some six miles west of the capital. According to Reuter (January 12, 1996), al-Jamri called for the restoration of the elected parliament and the release of detainees, in particular one Shaikh Muhammad al-Rayyash: "What crime has he committed? Is discussing constitutional demands a crime for which one detains another?"

his father and sister.[156] Then they took me to search my office. They took some files, and my computer. Then we went to the Ministry of Interior headquarters. Adil Flaifil told me, "OK, Ahmad, you've broken the law with this petition." The next day they demanded I apologize to the government for some of my newspaper articles. I refused.[157]

Shamlan's case went to the security court in mid-April. The charge sheet, according to Shamlan, consisted of an April 1995 article of his that appeared in the London-based Arabic daily *Al-Quds*, copies of faxes from the Bahrain Freedom Movement in London, a record of a telephone call from Mansur al-Jamri in London, and the statement of the Popular Petition Committee. Probably owing to Shamlan's high profile in the region and internationally, the security court, in an unusual move, released him on bail after its second hearing, in mid-April, and in May 1996 acquitted him of the charges.

Persons active in the petition movement calling for elections and restoration of the National Assembly have been dismissed from government jobs and in some cases blacklisted from finding other employment. Sa`id al-Asboul, an engineer, had been active in the petition campaign since 1991. In November 1994 he was dismissed from his job with the Ministry of Electricity and Public Works after refusing to withdraw his signature from the "popular" petition then being circulated. Subsequently the authorities reportedly intervened with the partly government-owned Aluminum Bahrain and with a British-owned company to prevent them from hiring al-Asboul.

Munira Fakhro, a professor of sociology at Bahrain University and one of the country's leading professional women, was suspended when she refused to retract her name from a petition which she and eight other women had initiated in

---

[156] Shamlan is one of Shaikh al-Jamri's lawyers. Mansur al-Jamri, his son, is active with the Bahrain Freedom Movement in London.

[157] Shamlan, who has published several volumes of poetry, has also been a columnist in *Al-Sharq* (Qatar), *Al-Khalij* (Sharjah) and *Al-Watan* (Kuwait). The column also appeared in 1993 and 1994 in one of Bahrain's two dailies, *Akhbar al-Khalij*. Shamlan told Human Rights Watch that his last column to appear in *Akhbar al-Khalij*, in December 1994, did not directly criticize the government but did suggest that local problems rather than outside forces lay behind the unrest that had broken out. He continued to send columns to the paper for several more months but none were published. The U.S. Department of State *Country Reports on Human Rights Practices for 1995* wrote that Shamlan "was suspended from his job after he signed a petition calling for a return to parliamentary democracy" (p.1131).

May 1995.[158] Two other signatories, Aziza Bassam, who worked for Bahrain Radio, and Hassa Khumairi, who was director of a literacy project for adult women in the Ministry of Education, were fired from their positions when they similarly refused. According to several participants who spoke with Human Rights Watch, the intent was to reiterate the main demands of the earlier petitions—elections, dialogue, and freedom for political prisoners—but also to call explicitly for the right of Bahraini women to participate in decision-making. "Within two weeks we got 311 signatures," one participant told Human Rights Watch, "and we contacted the amir's secretary right away for a meeting. A week later, when we never heard back from them, we sent it by DHL."[159] According to Fakhro, some ninety-two of the signatories worked for the government—most of them teachers.[160] A month or so later, Fakhro told Human Rights Watch, the heads of departments in the various ministries began contacting those women working under them to demand that they retract their signatures and apologize to the government. Of the fifty or sixty women contacted, all except Fakhro, Bassam and Khumairi acceded.[161] One woman who felt compelled by the threat of the loss of her job to retract her name told Human Rights Watch that she and other women were first asked to write individual letters of apology. When few did so, the Ministry of Education forwarded a form letter to sign. "We refused," this person said, "and they have not pursued this. Of course, all of us who signed in the first place still support the demands. Women we

---

[158] Ambassador Abdul Ghaffar, responding to questions submitted by Human Rights Watch, wrote: "With regard to Munira Fakhro and Sa`id Asbool, I can assure you they were properly dismissed for abuses of their positions and acts incompatible with their professional responsibilities. Their dismissals were not for exercising their rights to freedom of expression." The ambassador does not, however, specify what those abuses and incompatible acts might have been.

[159] Human Rights Watch interview, May 1996.

[160] Human Rights Watch interview, Washington, D.C., November 1995.

[161] Aziza Bassam subsequently went to work for *Akhbar al-Khalij*, one of Bahrain's two main dailies. Munira Fakhro and Hassa Khumairi lived outside Bahrain since losing their positions; Fakhro returned to Bahrain in early 1997 but has refused to write the apology the government is demanding as the price for getting back her teaching position.

thought would oppose the petition signed it, and many others who were afraid to sign told us it spoke for them."[162]

Several Bahrainis active in the broader petition campaign have told Human Rights Watch that since December 1994 hundreds of persons have been dismissed from their jobs, ostensibly on the grounds that signing a public petition demanding political reform is incompatible with their status as government employees, and that few have been reinstated.[163]

Human Rights Watch received a report that Dr. Zahra Isa al-Zira, a faculty member in the College of Education, was forced to resign from her position by the president of Bahrain University, Colonel Muhammad Jasim al-Ghatam, for comments she had made to students regarding Bahraini politics.[164] According to the Committee on Academic Freedom of the Middle East Studies Association of North America, Dr. al-Zira was summoned by the president of the university on January 20, 1997, and ordered to resign on the grounds of views she had allegedly expressed to students regarding the political situation in the country. When she resisted the order she was reportedly told that the alternative was referral to the SIS.[165]

On March 6, 1997, Sayyid Jalal Sayyid `Alawi Sayyid Sharaf, a telecommunications engineer employed by BATELCO, the national telecommunications company, was arrested in a dawn raid on his home, and his home computer equipment was confiscated. As of early May, his family still remained ignorant of his whereabouts and his condition. The authorities have not announced or given any reason for his arrest, although, according to Amnesty International, "he may be suspected by the authorities of transmitting information

---

[162] Human Rights Watch interview, Manama, June 1996. On the women's petition, see the letter to Amir Isa from Human Rights Watch/Middle East ("Bahrain: Harassment of Pro-democracy Women Activists," October 12, 1995).

[163] Human Rights Watch interviews, Manama, June 1996.

[164] Bahrain Human Rights Organization, "Attacks on Freedom of Expression," January 31, 1997; Amnesty International Urgent Action (AI Index: UA 54/97), February 20, 1997.

[165] Letter of the committee to Amir Isa, March 18, 1997. "Such cases have created an environment of terror in academic circles," the committee wrote, "promoting self censorship and acquiescence, and subsequently an unhealthy academic setting." The letter also protests university discrimination against Shi`a students and collective punishment of students and teachers at the secondary level.

about the internal situation in Bahrain to persons abroad through the Internet system."[166]

Freedom of the Press

Broadcast media is controlled directly by the government, and a combination of state censorship and self-censorship rules out serious discussion of internal politics in any print media. Amiri Decree 14/1979 With Respect to Publications, along with the relevant provisions of the 1976 Penal Code, forms the statutory basis for government control of the press.[167] Article 15 authorizes the Ministry of Information to ban the circulation of publications "which include any offense to the system of government in the State...." Article 40(b) proscribes "making any criticism of or blaming the Amir for any act of government or holding him responsible for any act." Article 42 would punish by imprisonment and fine those who publish "any offense" against any head of state maintaining diplomatic relations with Bahrain or "any scorn or contempt" of legislative councils, courts, or judicial bodies, while Article 43 punishes publication of "any news reports which may adversely affect the value of the national currency or caus[e] confusion with respect to the country's economic position...." Reporters, columnists, editors, and others involved in newspaper production must obtain work permits from the Ministry of Information (Article 23). Article 64 mandates the same for foreign correspondents, and adds:

> The Minister of Information may serve a warning to any correspondent of any foreign newspaper, magazine or news agency if it is found that the reports published imply any exaggeration, invention, misrepresentation or distortion. Should such [an] act recur, the permit given thereto may be withdrawn....

Article 37 authorizes the Ministry of Information to establish a Film and Recorded Matter Censorship Committee which "shall have the membership of representatives from a number of relevant ministries."

---

[166] Amnesty International Urgent Action, March 25, 1997.

[167] This decree was published in issue number 1344 of the Official Gazette, August 16, 1979.

In June 1993, the authorities closed down the Bahrain office of the UAE-based magazine *Al-Shuruq* when the bureau chief refused to provide the original transcript of an interview with an opposition figure.[168] None of the several petitions, for instance, including the one which supporters claim has secured some 25,000 signatures, has ever been published in Bahrain. Circulation of the petitions have been entirely by hand and by fax, according to Bahrainis interviewed by Human Rights Watch. One Bahraini journalist formerly with one of the country's two major dailies, and now working outside the country, told Human Rights Watch that informal constraints on publishing news and opinion about local political developments in Bahrain have grown considerably over the past decade.[169] This reporter told Human Rights Watch that the editor of the newspaper and the minister of information separately warned that Saudi officials had complained about the reporter's articles. "Today anything I write is 'too much,'" this person said.[170]

The government has interfered with the broadcast of BBC programs reflecting views critical of its policies and has arrested Bahrainis for speaking with visiting journalists. In April 1996, for example, following the visit of BBC Middle East correspondent Simon Ingram, Sa'id al-Asboul was detained without charge for a week and interrogated about who had arranged meetings for Ingram.[171] In May 1996, a Bahraini taxi driver and an Omani resident married to a Bahraini were detained and reportedly tortured under interrogation for accompanying BBC

---

[168] Committee to Protect Journalists, *Attacks on the Press in 1993* (New York: Committee to Protect Journalists, 1994), p. 217.

[169] The tenor of Bahrain's main print media can be gleaned from the lead in *Al-Ayam* following the government announcement that it had uncovered the Iran-backed "Hizballah Bahrain-Military Wing" plot: "There is nothing more pleasing than a proud and lofty homeland and seeing citizens renewing their allegiance to [Amir] Isa, the leader and father—glorious Isa" (as broadcast on Bahrain's state radio, Foreign Broadcast Information Service, Near East and South Asia [hereinafter FBIS-NES], June 5, 1996).

[170] Human Rights Watch interview, May 1996. When the government announced in early June 1996 that it had uncovered an Iranian-sponsored plot against the state, the two daily newspapers devoted virtually their entire issues for several days to amplifications of the government's story in its news and opinion columns and ran dozens of pages of full-page advertisements from various companies and social clubs and organizations congratulating the amir and the prime minister for their vigilance.

[171] Amnesty International issued a number of Urgent Actions at the time of al-Asboul's detention.

television reporter Sue Lloyd Roberts. The Omani, Abd al-Jalil al-Usfur, was released after three months and deported; the Bahraini, Sayyid Hussain, was reportedly released a short while later.

Foreign journalists themselves have also been the targets of government disapproval, especially when it comes time to renew their residency permits.[172] The renewal application of the Reuter correspondent based in Manama was rejected in March 1994, and Agence France-Presse, the other international agency that had a permanent presence in Manama, has also pulled out. Reuter, AFP and Associated Press presently cover Bahrain developments from Dubai and Nicosia. Locally based correspondents for international news agencies have also experienced government attempts at intimidation. In September 1996, Abbas Salman, a forty-seven-year-old Bahraini journalist working for Reuter since 1977, was detained for more than twenty-four hours and interrogated about a story he had written; he was released without charges.[173] In 1995, a newly-arrived correspondent for a European press agency was reportedly called into the Ministry of Information following a dispatch that quoted someone from the opposition.[174] On April 4, 1995, *Al-Ayam*, one of Bahrain's two mass-circulation Arabic dailies, published a statement by then-Minister of Information Tariq al-Mu`ayyad reiterating the need for foreign correspondents to get official accreditation, and adding:

> The ministry wishes to draw attention to the fact that it is prohibited for any citizen to send news to the outside without obtaining permission from the ministry. The ministry likes to stress that it is keen not to let the citizens be embarrassed, because any news attributed to them will lead to their legal questioning.[175]

---

[172] According to Article 19 (see above), the Ministry of Information issues visas as well as accreditation for foreign journalists.

[173] Reuter, "Bahrain detains Reuter newsman for over 24 hours," September 22, 1996.

[174] According to Article 19, any attempt to bypass the Ministry of Information can lead to the withdrawal of press credentials and, in the case of a foreign correspondent, revocation of a visa.

[175] Cited in Article 19, unpublished report (typescript), p. 22.

Bahrainis who try to circumvent media restrictions inside the country and who lack the international profile of a person like Ahmad al-Shamlan are treated harshly. Mahdi Rabea, a secondary school teacher and freelance contributor to the Bahrain daily *Al-Ayam* and the London-based magazine *Al-'Alam*, was arrested on December 20, 1995, and accused of drafting and distributing opposition leaflets. At his first hearing before the security court, he reportedly complained, to no avail, that he had confessed under torture. He was subsequently convicted under Article 168 of the Penal Code and sentenced to six months in prison, including time served.[176] In July 1996 Sultan Ali Abdallah Sultan, was similarly sentenced by the security court to six months "on charges of distributing false news and rumors."[177]

On February 16, 1997, Ali Hasan Yusif, who had been dismissed a few weeks earlier from his job with the Ministry of Information, was arrested, apparently in connection with a volume of poems he had published a year earlier. Yusif, a writer and freelance journalist, had worked at the ministry for some fifteen years, where he was responsible for reviewing and censoring films, according to family members, and he had not had any previous encounters with the authorities.[178] His book, *Isharat* (Symbols), had reportedly been cleared for distribution at the time of publication, but a Ministry of Information official told Agence France-Presse prior to his arrest that he had been dismissed "for infringing the law on publications" and that he was being questioned by the "competent authorities, like any other citizen who breaks the law and regulations of the country."[179]

---

[176] International Freedom of Expression (IFEX) Action Alerts, April 17 and May 14, 1996; Reuter, "Journalist among 14 jailed in Bahrain," April 16, 1996. On Article 168, see above.

[177] Reuter, July 4, 1976.

[178] Human Rights Watch telephone interview, February 1997.

[179] "Bahraini official sacked for criticizing country's situation," January 30, 1997. Yusif was released on April 15, 1997, after paying a find of BD 300 ($800). According to the bulletin of the Bahrain Freedom Movement (April 17, 1997), Abd al-Karim Yusif Mardi had been jailed for the previous six weeks for allegedly disseminating poetry critical of the government.

Forced Exile

Bahrain stands apart in the Middle East, and very nearly in the world, in its flagrantly illegal practice of forcibly exiling its own citizens, in violation of Article 13 (2) of the Universal Declaration of Human Rights and Article 17 (c) of Bahrain's constitution, which unequivocally states, "No citizen shall be deported from Bahrain, nor shall he be denied re-entry." Human Rights Watch has spoken with Bahrainis who were forcibly exiled recently, as well as with some who have been kept outside their country for two decades and longer. In 1992 and 1993, an undetermined number of Bahrainis living abroad were informally encouraged to return, and in 1994 the U.S. State Department reported that twenty-one exiles had been amnestied and they and their families given permission to return.[180] The practice of forced exile and preventing citizens from returning nevertheless continues. Most estimates place at 500 the number of forcibly exiled Bahrainis and their family members presently outside the country involuntarily.[181]

The practice of forced exile does enjoy some measure of precedent, as it was utilized on numerous occasions by British authorities, and virtually every period of unrest in Bahrain's modern history included the forced exile of key figures. But the practice enjoys no sanction in law whatsoever, or in legal

---

[180] U.S. Department of State, *Country Reports on Human Rights Practices for 1994*, p. 1056. The State Department report also noted that an undetermined number of Bahrainis who attempted to exercise their right to return were turned away at the airport during the same time period. The *Country Report* for 1992 stated that "an amnesty was decreed for Bahraini exiles living abroad" (p. 984), failing to note that it was quite limited in scope.

[181] This figure of 500 is now used in the latest U.S. Department of State *Country Reports*, citing Bahraini emigre sources; earlier reports used a much lower estimate of between 100 and 150. In 1994 the International Commission of Jurists cited reports from the Federation Internationale des Ligues des Droits de l'Homme, whose Bahraini affiliate is the Damascus-based Committee for the Defense of Human Rights in Bahrain, that around 600 Bahraini families were affected by this practice and that, according to the CDHRB, 128 nationals had been forcibly expelled in 1993 alone (ICJ, *The Review* no.52/1994, p. 1). According to a reliable independent Bahraini exile source (communication, May 1997), approximately 100 Bahraini citizens, all males, have been themselves forcibly deported by the government. There are some 400 spouses and children—"deportees by association"—who in a number of cases have been denied re-entry into Bahrain on the basis of their relationship with their exiled husband or father. The number of Bahraini *biduun* who have been forcibly exiled is not known, but appears to be of a similar order of magnitude. Between 200 and 300 other Bahraini citizens and residents remain abroad because of perceived threats to their personal integrity should they return.

procedure, and is invoked by the authorities in a completely arbitrary fashion, for no stated reason and without any semblance of a hearing. Bahraini defense lawyers told Human Rights Watch that the government makes no effort to justify its practice of forced exile on legal grounds.[182]

The most recent forced expulsions, to Human Rights Watch's knowledge, involved Shaikh Ali Salman and six others who were exiled in January 1995, at the outset of the current unrest. According to Salman:

> Around December 22 [1994], Adil Flaifil returned to question me again about the petition. If you withdraw your name, he told me, this will all be finished. I refused. A week later I was taken from the CID headquarters to Manama prison. I was put alone in cell number thirty-one. On the last morning, I was told to collect my things and taken to see Adil Flaifil, who told me they were going to deport me. He told me to choose Syria, Iran or Lebanon. I refused. He said they would send me to Syria via Dubai. They brought me to a special hall at the airport. Shaikh Hamza was there too, and British plainclothesmen, Henderson's crew.[183]

---

[182] The unequivocal constitutional right of a Bahraini citizen to return is to some extent undermined by Article 15 of the Passport Law of 1975, which gives the minister of interior discretion to refuse to renew passports and travel documents (International Commission of Jurists, *The Review* no.52/1994, p.4). Human Rights Watch is not aware of any instance where Bahraini authorities have invoked the Passport Law in order to justify their arbitrary and illegal policy of denying citizens permission to return.

[183] Human Rights Watch interview, London, March 1996. A high-ranking British official then stationed in Bahrain told Human Rights Watch that the "British plainclothesmen" observed by Shaikh Ali may well have been attached to airport security rather than to the Special Intelligence Service (interview, London, March 1996). Bahrainis who have attempted to re-enter the country told Human Rights Watch that Henderson has his own people at the airport. "They are known by the deference they receive from the others," said exiled sociologist Abd al-Hadi Khalaf. "One will sit passively at all formal interviews with people who have some problems at the airport."

Salman, Shaikh Hamza al-Dairi, and Shaikh Haidar al-Sitri managed to get to London, where they received asylum and now reside. At the time Crown Prince Hamad bin Isa Al Khalifa criticized the U.K. for allowing itself to become a "haven for terrorists and

The post-Gulf war amnesties allowing some exiles to return were limited in number and included no prominent opposition activists.[184] One Bahraini told Human Rights Watch that he had left Bahrain to study in Lebanon and later in the Soviet Union in the mid-1970s. When he attempted to return in December 1992, he spent twenty hours at the airport, was given a one-year passport, and told not to return until a general amnesty had been decreed.[185]

Jamal Habib Umran, thirty years old, now living in Dubai, had left the country in 1979 to get medical treatment in the Soviet Union, and while abroad he became active in the General Union of Bahraini Students, an "unauthorized" group. Umran told Human Rights Watch about his attempt to return in 1991:

> The immigration officer at the airport checked the computer and told me to take a seat. Some special security men interrogated me. Why have you come? Because I am a citizen, I said. It is my constitutional right. What have you been doing? Why are you returning after all this time? I told them I had the impression that things were better, that I'd heard about the amnesty, although since I had not worked against the security of the state it did not really apply to me. Eventually I insisted on speaking to Ian Henderson or some other top security official. I refused to respond to these low-level bureaucrats.

Umran spent the night under guard at the airport. "I had brought a small bag with a toothbrush," he said, "expecting this scene." In the morning a different official came to the airport. "Look," he told Umran, "no one wants to see you. Take your passport and go back where you came from."

---

saboteurs," and other Bahraini officials were quoted in the Arab press as warning of "negative consequences" for Britain if asylum were granted ("Bahrain Anger and Islamists in U.K.," *The Guardian*, January 27, 1995).

The Bahrain Human Rights Organization in February 1995 issued a list of twenty-two persons exiled during January 1995 (DK 9502144, 14 February 1995).

[184] The Bahrain Human Rights Organization in December 1994 published a list of 211 persons, including children, who had been denied the right to enter Bahrain over the previous four years, with date of return and country to which they were deported (DK 9412152, 15 December 1994).

[185] Human Rights Watch interview, Dubai, June 1996.

> My family was in the waiting room. I took out a white sheet and wrapped myself as in a shroud and lay down in the transit lounge. They carried me into another room. If you pulled this behavior in your home, they said, your father would not like it. Yes, but he would let me in, I replied. If I did something wrong, put me on trial. They prepared my new passport. I refused to sign the application. They asked my family for money to send me back, but I had already told them to come to the airport without money. They carried me to a Gulf Air plane. I told the steward I was on board against my will and I wanted to talk to the pilot. He said OK, but next thing I knew the door was shut and the plane was taking off. I stood up and told the other passengers what had happened, that I was being deported with a one-year passport.

In Dubai, Umran called his family, had them wire him money, and bought a ticket for the next flight to Bahrain.

> At Bahrain immigration they put me back on the plane to Dubai. There I bought another ticket and tried again. This time they said that each time I tried to come back would mean two years of additional exile. After this third time, my brother told me the family could not afford to buy me any more tickets.[186]

Abd al-Hadi Khalaf had been elected to the National Assembly in 1973, but his election was ruled invalid on the grounds that he was then not yet thirty years old. He was detained in June 1974, in connection with the workers' strike at the Aluminum Bahrain plant (see above), and held without charge for seven months. After being arrested again in December 1975, he was held without charge until the following May. "For a while I was in a cell right across from Henderson's office," he told Human Rights Watch. "He agreed to meet with me, and when I asked why I was being held he replied that it was politics, not security, and therefore not his business."[187] Khalaf left Bahrain following his release. When he attempted to return in March 1992, he was interrogated at the airport and

---

[186] Human Rights Watch interview, Dubai, June 1996.

[187] Human Rights Watch interview, London, August 1996.

dispatched back to London. "It must be said," he wrote afterwards in an open letter to Amir Isa:

> that the security men who interrogated me were polite.... The
> two Arab officers could barely conceal their shame at the task
> they had been ordered to perform. All they did was translate into
> Arabic the questions which were written down in English.[188]

Khalaf, who now teaches sociology in Sweden, also wrote that he had offered to answer any legal charges connected with this "exercise of the constitutional right to oppose unconstitutional policies."

Abdallah Rashid had been active with the National Liberation Front of Bahrain and was forcibly exiled twice, for brief periods, under the British, in 1960 (for distributing leaflets and writing wall slogans) and again in 1970. In 1974, after independence, he was detained from June to October and subsequently expelled. In 1993 he and two others flew back via Yemen.

> I only had an expired passport. We were there just fifteen
> minutes, and they told us we had to get out. We refused. They
> tried to force us back on the plane, telling the pilot we were
> Palestinians! I told the pilot who we really were, and that it was
> his responsibility under international rules of aviation not to
> comply with their order. Finally security relented and brought us
> to the terminal, each of us in a separate car surrounded by six
> heavily armed police. We were then taken to the old airport
> where we were kept in separate brightly lit rooms for a week.
> Then Henderson came, just back from London. "What do you
> want?" he asked. "Just to return to my country," I said. "Will
> you do political work?" he asked. "It is allowed in the
> constitution," I replied. They interrogated me a second day. In
> the end, they said I had to go back. The day before leaving, they
> brought me a report about myself, my activities from 1958 till
> then, to read. Some of it was right, some of it wrong. They took

---

[188] Khalaf's open letter to Amir Isa appeared in *Al-Quds al-Arabi* (London), April 28, 1992, and was excerpted in *Mideast Mirror* (London), April 28, 1992.

us to the plane blindfolded. They never said why we couldn't stay.[189]

Forced exile means more than simply not being able to go home. Abdallah Rashid's account of life in forced exile was echoed by others with whom Human Rights Watch spoke:

I can only get a passport good for a year at a time. This means I can't get a residence permit for more than a year. This means you cannot commit yourself to an employer for more than ten months at a time, which makes it very difficult to be hired. A lot of us are in this situation. And our passports are good for travel to only one or maybe two or three other countries. So we can't travel and can't get jobs.[190]

Among Bahrainis forcibly exiled are some who are *biduun*—without nationality (see above). Many were expelled, and others fled, in the early and mid-1980s, following the Iranian revolution and government charges of Iranian-sponsored attempts to seize power by the Islamic Front for the Liberation of Bahrain.

[189] Human Rights Watch interview, Beirut, May 1996.

[190] Human Rights Watch interview, Beirut, May 1996.

6. THE ROLE OF THE INTERNATIONAL COMMUNITY

The Arab World

The government of Bahrain enjoys the unreserved public support of most Arab governments of the Persian Gulf, particularly in the forum of the Gulf Cooperation Council (GCC). Saudi Arabia, Kuwait and the United Arab Emirates reportedly resumed annual subsidies of $50 million each to Bahrain's rulers following the onset of the political unrest at the end of 1994.[191] None of these governments have criticized Bahrain's human rights practices, with the exception of Qatar which, in December 1996, criticized the security court trial in Bahrain of two Qatari nationals charged with spying (see below).

After a meeting of the GCC interior ministers in Manama in mid-April 1995, GCC Secretary-General Fahim al-Qassimi declared that the GCC states "stand by Bahrain and fully support measures taken to maintain security and stability.... The GCC states denounce the phenomenon of extremism...and are determined to fight this destructive phenomenon which is alien to Islam."[192] On June 2, 1996, one day before Bahrain announced it had uncovered "a serious conspiracy" by a previously unknown organization, Hizb Allah Bahrain-Military Wing, "to overthrow the Bahrain government and replace it with a pro-Iranian regime," the GCC foreign ministers convened to condemn Iran for interfering "in the internal affairs of Bahrain and other member countries."[193] The Arab heads of state, at a summit a few weeks later devoted mainly to Arab-Israeli relations following the election of Binyamin Netanyahu as prime minister of Israel, included in their final communique a paragraph expressing "their complete support for the measures [Bahrain] has taken to strengthen security and stability."[194]

Saudi Arabia in particular has supported Bahrain's rulers with regard to the internal unrest. Prince Nayif, the Saudi minister of interior, following a November 1995 meeting of GCC interior ministers, told reporters that, "Saudi

---

[191] Reuter, June 1, 1995.

[192] Reuter, April, 19, 1995.

[193] Press and wire service reports cited in Cordesman, pp. 44-45. The GCC meeting was preceded by U.S. public statements and private demarches declaiming Iran's military buildup and hostile intent in the Gulf. See, for example, the discussion in *Mideast Mirror*, June 4, 1996.

[194] The text of the final communique appeared in *Mideast Mirror*, June 24, 1996.

Arabia will not hesitate at any time in responding to any request from Bahrain...and the security of Saudi Arabia and Bahrain together will be for the service of the Bahraini people."[195] Prince Sultan, the Saudi minister of defense, told the BBC in March that, "We are prepared to stand forcefully by Bahrain if the need arises."[196] After the unrest began in December 1994, Saudi Arabia increased Bahrain's allotment from a shared offshore oil field from 70,000 to 100,000 barrels a day. In late March 1996, following a resumption and intensification of the unrest, Bahrain was granted the entire production of 140,000 barrels per day.[197] The Bahrain Defense Force "has held cooperative exercises with Saudi forces designed to demonstrate that it could count on Saudi support" and has "discussed contingency plans for Saudi military assistance."[198]

The Kuwaiti government has also frequently expressed solidarity with Bahrain's rulers, but in February 1996 a delegation of eight Kuwaiti parliamentarians attempted to visit Bahrain to deliver a petition signed by about one hundred of their colleagues urging Amir Isa to negotiate with the opposition. They were turned back at the airport.[199] On May 14, 1996, Kuwaiti security officials detained Jamil Abd al-Ghani Abdallah Ali, a twenty-five-year-old Bahraini working in a Kuwaiti government social security office, and, with no

---

[195] "Bahrain: Saudi in Security Pledge," *Egyptian Gazette*, November 13, 1995.

[196] Interview with the Arabic Service of the BBC, as cited in *Mideast Mirror*, March 28, 1997.

[197] "Bahrain execution sparks rioting," *Financial Times*, March 27, 1996.

[198] Cordesman, p. 107. According to the Washington correspondent of *The Sunday Times* (London), James Adams, "In military manouevres, Saudi Arabia has practiced an assault on a fundamentalist Bahrain and it is clear the Saudis are prepared to take action if Bahrain were to fall to Iranian-backed revolutionaries" (June 9, 1996).

The Saudi ruling family has a reputation for hostility to elections in the Persian Gulf and Arabian Peninsula. "At a January meeting in Tunisia, the Saudi interior minister, Prince Nayif, urged his Yemeni counterpart to cancel the parliamentary elections [scheduled for late April 1997] as a threat to stability in the region, according to a senior Yemeni official and Western diplomats" (*Washington Post*, April 26, 1997).

[199] This incident also prompted a statement of parliamentarians supporting the Bahraini government, who then visited Bahrain and met with the amir (Reuter, February 13, 1996).

judicial or administrative proceedings, turned him over to Bahraini authorities at the Saudi-Kuwaiti border.[200] In the aftermath of Bahrain's announcement of the alleged Hizb Allah Bahrain coup, the Kuwaiti parliament issued a statement supporting the Bahraini government concerning "the unfortunate incidents that have taken place recently," but pointedly refrained from mentioning, much less condemning, Iran.[201] In late March 1997, Kuwaiti authorities detained eleven Bahraini nationals for "gathering donations without permission and distributing illegal literature."[202] Other arrests of Bahrainis followed, and as of April 29 seven were still being held for further investigation.[203]

Bahrain's relations with Qatar have been strained for a number of years owing to a long-standing dispute over the Hawar islands lying between the two countries. Relations worsened after the Qatari crown prince, Shaikh Hamad bin Khalifa, deposed his father in June 1995, took control of the government, and was soon recognized by governments in the region and internationally. Qatar's ex-ruler, Shaikh Khalifa bin Hamad Al Thani, continued to claim the throne. After Bahrain received him as if he were still head of state, Qatar's new ruler retaliated by allowing Bahraini opposition figures to broadcast appeals for elections in Bahrain over Qatari airwaves. Relations between the two countries reached their nadir in December 1996, when Bahrain refused to attend a scheduled GCC summit meeting in Doha and brought to trial two Qataris resident in Bahrain on charges of

---

[200] After inquiries from Abd al-Ghani's wife and from members of the human rights committee in Kuwait's parliament, the Ministry of Interior finally acknowledged its failure to follow elementary extradition procedures in this case. Human Rights Watch interview with Ali al-Baghli, member of parliament, Kuwait, May 1996.

[201] According to *Al-Hayat*'s Kuwait correspondent, as summarized in *Mideast Mirror*, June 12, 1996.

[202] *Al-Watan* (Kuwait), March 31, 1997, as cited in Amnesty International Urgent Action of April 2, 1997 (AI Index: MDE 17/01/97). The Urgent Action also cites a claim in the Bahraini daily *Al-Ayam* (April 2) that those detained "had distributed videotapes and pamphlets harmful to the security of Bahrain and other Gulf states."

[203] Agence France-Presse, "Bahraini released in Kuwait, seven still held," April 29, 1997.

spying.[204] Fahd Ahmad al-Bakir and Salwa Jasim were convicted before a security court and sentenced to three-year prison terms and fines of approximately $2,650 each.[205] The crisis eased somewhat several days later when the Bahraini ruler granted the two pardons.

Oman has also been publicly supportive of the government of Bahrain. In May 1996, however, Sultan Qabus told *Al-Hayat*, "A person must advise his brother. I believe that the government of Bahrain understands its affairs and it will overcome the crisis because it is an internal crisis. The solution must be internal."[206]

Among Arab governments outside the Gulf, Jordan and Egypt have been most openly supportive of Bahrain. An unknown number of Jordanian officers serve with the Bahrain Defense Forces and also with the country's security and intelligence services.[207] In March 1996, in response to a question about the possibility that Jordan might send troops to Bahrain, Jordan's then-Prime Minister Abd al-Karim al-Kabariti declared that his government "is prepared to provide all political, moral and material support" and that it was up to Bahrain's rulers to "choose the form of support it is seeking from Jordan," adding that Bahrain had not submitted such a request.[208]

Iran

The government of Bahrain, while maintaining that its policies do not violate human rights, has repeatedly invoked fear of Iranian subversion to justify its restrictions on the exercise of civil and political rights in the country. As noted in the historical background section of this report, the Al Khalifa ruling family established its own legitimacy in contestation with Iranian claims of sovereignty

---

[204] According to a Reuter account, "[i]t was unclear when the two were arrested, but a source close to the court said they were detained about five months ago" (Reuter, "Bahrain Court Jails Two Accused Qatari Spies," December 25, 1996).

[205] Bahrain government radio (WAKH), translated in FBIS-NES, December 25, 1996.

[206] May 28, 1996, as reported by the Bahrain Freedom Movement, May 29, 1996.

[207] According to Cordesman (p. 101), the BDF "has suffered from the loss of a number of Jordanian officers and personnel...as a result of Jordan's support of Iraq during the Gulf War."

[208] *Al-Hayat*, March 24, 1996. According to one estimate, some thirty Jordanian officers are stationed in Manama (Compass Newswire, May 2, 1996).

over Bahrain. Iran formally withdrew those claims in negotiations with Great
Britain, a process facilitated by a UN-sponsored "consultation" establishing that
most Bahrainis preferred independence to Iranian rule.

Iran's claims were briefly reasserted in speeches by the new clerical
leadership from Tehran following the 1979 revolution. Of greater concern to
Bahrain's rulers was the appeal of Iran's revolutionary example to Bahrain's Shi`a
majority population, which produced demonstrations, arrests and expulsions in
support of the Islamic Republic and, after September 1980, in opposition to
Bahrain's support for Iraq's military attack on Iran. In mid-December 1981,
Bahraini authorities arrested some 73 people, 58 of them Bahrainis, whom it
accused of planning a coup in the name of the Islamic Front for the Liberation of
Bahrain. The accused were tried before the security court and many were sentenced
to long prison terms. Some 300 other persons, many of whom were *biduun* of
Iranian origin, were forcibly exiled or fled out of fear that they would be
apprehended on the basis of incriminating confessions by those in detention.[209] In
the course of other arrests, trials, and expulsions during the 1980s, the Bahrain
government reiterated charges of Iranian involvement.

Bahraini charges of Iranian support for Shi`a opposition forces in the
country resumed with the outbreak of unrest in December 1994, citing in particular
young Bahraini clerics who had attended theological schools in the Iranian city of
Qom.[210] For the most part these charges vaguely referred to "foreign interference"
without mentioning Iran by name.[211] In late January 1996, Bahrain expelled Abd
al-Rasul Dukuuhki, third secretary in Iran's embassy in Manama, for "activities and
practices incompatible with his diplomatic status," but ruled out severing ties with
Tehran on the grounds that such a decision should be taken by the GCC countries

---

[209] On those who endured forced exile, see above. For one account of the
December 1981 round-up, see Cordesman, pp. 42-43. Amnesty International, in its annual
report issued in 1987, cited the reported death from torture in Jaw prison of Radhi Ibrahim,
who had been sentenced to fifteen years in prison in this case.

[210] Historically Bahrain's Shi`a community had been oriented towards the
theological schools in Najaf, Iraq, but in the aftermath of Iraq's invasion of Kuwait in 1990
that venue has remained closed.

[211] For instance, then-Minister of Information Tariq al-Mu`ayyad told the *Wall
Street Journal* that discontent was restricted to "a small number of people" who "received
instructions from outside" ("Riots in Bahrain arouse ire of feared monarchy," June 12,
1995).

together.[212] In early June 1996, as noted above, the authorities announced that they had secured confessions from detainees confirming that Hizb Allah Bahrain, a group allegedly established at the behest of Iran's Islamic Revolutionary Guard Corps, had "since the end of 1994 aimed at terrorizing citizens and residents, and destabilizing Bahrain's security and stability."[213] Bahrain withdrew its ambassador from Tehran. According to Information Minister Muhammad al-Mutawwa'a, "The movement's main aims are to stage an armed revolution to overthrow the Bahrain government by force and to replace it with a pro-Iranian regime."[214] As it has on other occasions, Iran denied the charges of interference in Bahraini affairs. Iranian state radio asserted, "The propaganda of the Bahraini officials is parallel to the propaganda policies of the West against the Islamic Republic of Iran."[215]

United States officials have publicly but vaguely endorsed Bahraini government charges of Iranian involvement in the unrest, but have privately indicated that they do not regard that unrest as chiefly a consequence of Iranian intervention.[216]

The United States

The United States has had a naval presence in Bahrain since 1949, when a three-warship Middle East Force (MEF) was headquartered there. In December 1971, the U.S. signed a lease for its MEF with the newly independent state.[217] Bahrain has accommodated U.S. requests for increased access to military facilities at various crisis points since then, notably following the Arab-Israeli war in October 1973 and the accompanying boycott of Arab oil producing states, during the so-called "tanker war" in 1987-88 when U.S. forces protected Iraqi oil

---

[212] Reuter, February 1, 1996; *Al-Hayat,* January 29, 1996, via BBC Monitoring Service, January 31, 1996.

[213] "Interior Ministry on arrest of 'Hizballah of Bahrain' group," Bahrain state radio (WAKH), FBIS-NES, June 3, 1996.

[214] "Bahrain arrests 29 in move to foil 'Iran-backed coup,'" *The Times,* June 4, 1996.

[215] Reuter, June 4, 1996.

[216] See below.

[217] Cordesman, p. 38.

shipments against Iranian attack, and during Operation Desert Storm following Iraq's invasion of Kuwait.[218] In 1991 the U.S. and Bahrain signed a ten-year bilateral security agreement. Since 1995 Bahrain has been the operational headquarters for the U.S. Navy's Fifth Fleet; fifteen U.S. warships are presently "home ported" and some 1,500 U.S. military personnel and dependents are stationed there.[219]

The U.S. accounted for $260 million in arms deliveries to Bahrain between 1979 and 1988, out of total arms deliveries of $625 million, and $700 million in arms deliveries in the 1988-1995 period, out of total deliveries of $800 million.[220] The State Department congressional presentation for fiscal year 1997 estimated U.S. military sales to Bahrain at $160 million in fiscal year 1996 and $330 million in 1997. The presentation for fiscal 1998 lowered the 1997 estimate to $78.8 million and provided a fiscal 1998 estimate of $201.2 million.[221] U.S. military assistance to Bahrain presently takes the form of grants of excess defense articles (EDA) and International Military Education and Training (IMET) funds. In fiscal 1996, the last year for which figures are available, Bahrain received EDA

---

[218] The MEF lease was officially terminated on October 20, 1973, but was quietly reinstated and expanded in the summer of 1975 and again in June 1977. However, Bahrain asked that the U.S. make the arrangements "informal" and the MEF headquarters became a "temporary duty administrative unit" until the mid-1980s, when military cooperation became more extensive and more open (Cordesman, p. 38). U.S. officials, in background discussions with Human Rights Watch (interviews, Washington, March 1996), have cited Bahrain's cooperation "when we needed them" to explain the U.S. public solidarity with the ruling family and the absence of any U.S. criticism of Bahrain's human rights performance outside of the chapter in the annual *Country Reports on Human Rights Practices*.

[219] Cordesman, pp. 38-39. The U.S. command site now comprises some twenty-three acres of administrative buildings ("Bahrain turmoil fails to disturb U.S. presence," *Defense News*, May 6 - 12, 1996, p. 16). According to a March 8, 1997, Associated Press dispatch from aboard the USS Kitty Hawk, "At any one time, the Gulf is crowded with 20 to 25 warships flying the Stars and Stripes—at least 12,000 sailors, including 5,000 aboard whatever carrier is on station."

[220] Arms Control and Disarmament Agency data for 1979-88 is from Cordesman, p. 91; 1988-95 data is from Richard F. Grimmett, *Conventional Arms Transfers to Developing Nations, 1988-1995* (Washington: Congressional Research Service, August 15, 1996), p.64, table 2H.

[221] U.S. Department of State, *Congressional Presentation for Foreign Operations, Fiscal Year 1998*, p. 655.

materials presently valued at $82.3 million, and was able to "lease" at no cost U.S. "defense articles" worth $12.7 million.[222] In May 1997, a former U.S. Navy frigate donated to Bahrain, and worth an estimated $56 million, set sail from Charleston, South Carolina, for Manama.[223] For fiscal year 1998 the Clinton administration requested $175,000 in IMET funds for Bahrain.[224]

In September 1995, eighteen members of Congress signed a letter to Bahrain's ambassador urging the government "to uphold international standards of human rights" and citing reports of "forced exiles, detentions without trials and deaths under torture."[225] The U.S. government, however, has consistently avoided opportunities to criticize Bahrain's abusive human rights record. Defense Secretary William Perry made several visits to Bahrain during 1996 but made no public comment on the human rights situation. Secretary of State Warren Christopher, meeting in Washington on March 8, 1996, with Crown Prince and Deputy Prime Minister Hamad bin Isa Al Khalifa and Foreign Minister Muhammad bin Mubarak Al Khalifa, said, "Bahrain is a good friend to the United States and an important defense partner of the United States in the Gulf region. We are committed to working together to advance our shared interest in security and stability across the Middle East."[226] State Department spokesperson Nicholas Burns stated that human rights did not arise in Secretary of State Christopher's meeting with the Crown Prince, but that "[t]he issue has come up numerous times in our relationship with Bahrain through Ambassador David Ransom and others."[227]

On January 25, 1996, Assistant Secretary of State Robert Pelletreau said that unrest in Bahrain "is brought about by a fairly high level of unemployment and some unrest in Bahrain's Shi`a community. It is urged on and promoted by Iran,

---

[222] *Congressional Presentation for Foreign Operations,* pp. 682 and 684. The acquired value of the EDA items was put at $168.2 million.

[223] Reuter, May 13, 1997.

[224] Actual IMET spending for Bahrain in fiscal 1996 was $108,000, and estimated spending for fiscal 1997 was $125,000 (U.S. Department of State, *Congressional Presentation for Foreign Operations, Fiscal Year 1998,* p. 566).

[225] The letter was dated September 28, 1995.

[226] U.S. State Department transcript.

[227] Transcript of U.S. State Department daily press briefing, March 8, 1996.

across the Persian Gulf.... [Bahrain's leaders] are dealing with it, in my view, in a responsible way that deserves our support." On May 7, 1996, Pelletreau, at the United States Information Agency Foreign Press Center, reiterated that Bahrain's difficulties "are sometimes fanned by flames from Iran.... We believe that the government is taking steps to address this situation and that the government deserves the support of its neighbors and other friends as it tries to deal with an ongoing difficult problem."[228] State Department officials responsible for monitoring Iran's role in the Persian Gulf, speaking off the record, told Human Rights Watch in early 1996 that they have seen no evidence of an important or an instigatory Iranian role in Bahrain's political unrest.[229] On August 8, 1996, responding to a written Congressional question from June 12 about the credibility of Bahrain's claims of Iranian responsibility, Assistant Secretary Pelletreau wrote:

> The roots of the unrest appear to be domestic and involve the desire for expanded political participation and increased employment and opportunities. Iran's involvement in terrorist activities in the region is well known. There is credible evidence that a small group of Bahraini militants with a stated aim of overthrowing the government had received assistance and training from Iran. Iran is known to have links to opposition personalities in Bahrain through its embassy and the Bahrain Studies Center in Qom.[230]

In late May 1996, Gen. John Shalikashvili, chairman of the Joint Chiefs of Staff, visited Bahrain, where he said, "We support Bahrain's efforts to ensure its

---

[228] *Mideast Mirror*, May 8, 1996.

[229] Human Rights Watch interviews, March 1996. Most Western press accounts have also taken the view that Iran is playing, at most, a supporting role. See, for example, "Unrest in Persian Gulf Isle of Bahrain has U.S. unsettled," *The Los Angeles Times*, May 15, 1996; "Protests Mount in Bahrain," *The Washington Post*, March 27, 1996; "Tiger By the Tail," *Time*, July 22, 1996. In contrast, the Washington correspondent for *The Guardian*, writing in December 1996, referred to "U.S. naval intelligence reports claim[ing that] Iranian influence was behind this year's wave of riots and demonstrations in Bahrain" ("Saudis feed U.S. mood for Iran reprisal," December 12, 1996).

[230] Partial transcript provided by the U.S. House of Representatives, Committee on International Relations, p. 83.

stability, and we continue to accuse Iran as a threat to the stability of the region."
[231] Two weeks later, following the purported confessions of alleged Iranian-backed
coup plotters (see above), Bahrain released portions of a letter from President
Clinton to Amir Isa which stated, "The U.S. fully supports your government and
sovereignty and safety of Bahrain's territories," and praised his expansion of an
appointed Consultative Council as reaffirming "your government's commitment
to economic and social development and political reconciliation."[232] In September
1996, Secretary Perry returned to Bahrain to arrange for the basing of twenty-three
additional U.S. Air Force F-16s for use in patrolling the southern Iraq "no-fly"
zone. In March 1997, Deputy Secretary of Defense John White visited Bahrain for
talks on military cooperation.[233]

Former President George Bush visited Bahrain in March 1996, and
publicly commended the authorities for their handling of the protests: "I salute the
government of Bahrain for preserving order and for guaranteeing for every
Bahraini citizen a secure environment."[234]

The sole public U.S. critiques of Bahrain's human rights record are the
Bahrain entries in the State Department's annual *Country Reports on Human Rights
Practices*. Since 1994, in contrast to earlier years, those entries have been

---

[231] "Bahrain detains 29 militants accused of Iran-backed coup plan," *Washington
Post*, June 4, 1996. According to Bahrain's state radio, Shalikashvili "expressed the United
States' support for all the measures taken by the Bahraini government to confront acts of
violence and sabotage and to safeguard the country's security and stability," (FBIS-NES,
May 30, 1996).

[232] "Clinton supports Bahrain over anti-government plot," Reuter, June 12, 1996.
In the first official U.S. comment on the alleged plot, State Department spokesperson Glyn
Davies said that Washington took the charges of Iranian involvement "very, very
seriously.... Iran's involvement with terrorist activities in the region is well-known, and of
course, it's also well-known that they've established links with oppositionist parties in
Bahrain" (*Mideast Mirror*, June 5, 1996).

[233] "Bahrain, U.S. discuss military cooperation," Agence France-Presse, March 18,
1997.

[234] Agence France-Presse, March 26, 1996. In the early 1990s, George W. Bush,
the president's son and presently governor of Texas, served on the board of Harken Energy
Corp., which in January 1990, "though it had never drilled a single well overseas or in
water," won a Bahrain government contract to drill wildcat wells in its offshore waters (*Wall
Street Journal*, December 6, 1991).

reasonably comprehensive and candid in describing the scope of Bahrain's restrictions on basic civil liberties and due process rights, although they tend to be general rather than specific and have understated the extent to which people have been detained for exercising the right of free speech as distinguished from participation in demonstrations and clashes with the authorities. The 1995 chapter, for instance, asserted misleadingly that Shaikh Abd al-Amir al-Jamri had been accused of "a wide variety of security-related crimes."[235] In fact, such accusations consisted of statements in the government-controlled press, mostly unattributed, and reflected a highly expansive definition of "security-related."

The entries have also gratuitously denigrated the human rights monitoring of the Copenhagen-based Bahrain Organization for Human Rights (BHRO) and the Damascus-based Committee for the Defense of Human Rights in Bahrain (CDHRB). The State Department report groups the BHRO and the CDHRB with the Bahrain Freedom Movement and the Islamic Front for the Liberation of Bahrain, which make no claim to being human rights organizations, and then dismisses them all as "viewed by many local observers as espousing a political, rather than a purely human rights, agenda."[236] The entry further mischaracterized them as "small numbers of emigres living in self-imposed exile," thus downplaying the government's extensive use of forcible exile to punish political dissidence. Rather than assessing directly their allegations of abuse, the report attacked the BHRO and the CDHRB by innuendo as having "reportedly received funding from sources hostile to the Al Khalifa regime."[237]

---

[235] This wording, from the 1995 *Country Reports* (p. 1134), is essentially unchanged in the 1996 version.

[236] Ambassador Abdul Ghaffar's response to Human Rights Watch asserts that "the BHRO is not a bona fide Human Rights Organization and is run by...a trained terrorist and fugitive from the 1981 failed armed coup...." He further asserts that the BHRO and the Committee for the Defense of Human Rights in Bahrain "are all one and the same thing, merely being different names used as fronts by the Denmark-based propaganda wing of the Islamic Front for the Liberation of Bahrain, formally also based in Damascus." He adds, "They also act in concert with militant Hizbollah propagandists based in London," referring to the Bahrain Freedom Movement.

[237] This wording, from the 1995 *Country Reports* (p. 1134), remains unchanged in the 1996 version.

APPENDIX

HUMAN RIGHTS WATCH
485 5th Avenue
New York, New York 10017
Telephone: (212)972-8400
Facsimile: (212)972-0905
E-mail: hrwnyc@hrw.org
Website: http://www.hrw.org

March 7, 1997

His Highness Shaikh 'Isa ibn Salman al-Khalifa
The Amir of Bahrain
The Amiri Court, Rifa'a Palace
PO BOX 555
Manama, Bahrain

His Highness Shaikh Muhammad ibn Khalida al-Khalifa
Prime Minister of Bahrain
PO BOX 13
Manama, Bahrain

via facsimile and courier c/o His Excellency Muhammad Abdul Ghaffar, Embassy of Bahrain

Your Excellencies:

I have addressed this letter to both of you, trusting that you will decide who are the most appropriate officials to respond. Please excuse my addressing you in English, and feel free to respond in Arabic.

As you may be aware via Ambassador Ghaffar, Human Rights Watch is preparing a report on human rights conditions in Bahrain. We are sending you in this letter a list of substantive questions which arise from our ongoing monitoring of human rights in Bahrain. We regret that, because the government of Bahrain has so far declined our requests for permission to conduct an official mission to your country, we were not able to meet with you to discuss these matters and solicit your views at an earlier stage in our investigation.

We do hope you will respond to these questions, which reflect the chief concerns of the report in preparation, so that official information and perspectives will be reflected fairly in the published report. In the case of allegations that you regard as false, we trust you will inform us accordingly. Where our information is correct but you feel we have mischaracterized the circumstances, we would also appreciate your perspective. We would welcome, moreover, your comment on any matters that you feel are relevant but are not covered by the questions that follow. We will make every effort to include all pertinent information you provide in our final report. In order for this to be possible, we request that your reply be received by us no later than April 7, 1997.

Human Rights Watch letter to the Government of Bahrain
March 7, 1997
Page 2

Questions for the Government of Bahrain

(1) Forced Exile
Human Rights Watch (HRW) has spoken with many Bahrainis who have been forcibly exiled from
Bahrain by the authorities, and have not been permitted to re-enter the country. HRW has also
interviewed numerous Bahraini citizens who traveled abroad, in most cases to study, and have not
been permitted to re-enter the country. These individuals recounted to HRW their efforts to return
and their experiences of being forcibly prevented, at the main airport, from entering the country. It
is generally believed that at least 500 Bahrainis, and perhaps twice that number, are presently outside
the country against their wishes.

To the best of our knowledge, individuals forced to leave Bahrain or denied re-entry are not
informed of any reasons in fact or in law for this action, and there is no semblance of legal procedure
or hearing. We would appreciate it if you could share with us your view of how this practice
comports with Bahrain's legal obligations, notably with regard to Article 13 of the Universal
Declaration of Human Rights and Article 17 of Bahrain's constitution, and we would welcome any
comments you may have concerning our observations on this point.

(2) Detention without trial or charges
Human Rights Watch has spoken with numerous Bahrainis who have testified that they have been
seized and detained without charges and without trial, for varying periods of time. HRW has also
spoken with a number of practicing Bahraini defense lawyers, all of whom assert that this occurs
frequently. The discrepancy between the large numbers of persons detained in 1996, for example,
and the small numbers convicted or released suggests that this may be a pattern.

We would appreciate receiving information regarding the legal and procedural safeguards against
prolonged detention without charge. If there have been instances of illegal detention, what measures
have been taken to punish those responsible? Can you please inform us of the number of persons
detained for security-related offenses since December 1994, the number of persons charged in the
security court or in the ordinary criminal court for such offenses, the number of persons convicted,
and the number of persons acquitted?

(3) Freedom of speech
Among those detained without charge or trial for a prolonged period are eight prominent members
of Bahrain's Shi`a community. On January 23, 1996, the Ministry of Interior announced that Abd
al-Amir al-Jamri, Abd al-Wahab al-Hussain, Hasan Mushaima, Ali Ahmad Howarah, Hasan Ali
Muhammad Sultan, Ibrahim Adnan Nasir al-Alawi, Abd al-Ashur al-Satrawi and Hussain Ali Hasan
al-Daihi were under arrest. At the time a government official asserted, "There is proof, evidence, and
documents supported by pictures which prove the group's involvement in the incidents [of violence]

and would be submitted to the legal authorities." Since that time, government spokespersons have made similar claims to the media, but none of these individuals has been formally charged or tried. They have not been allowed to see lawyers or have regular access to family members. We are unaware of any evidence that any of these individuals has engaged in or advocated violence. From information available to us, it appears that they may have been detained merely for expressing their political views and for advocating the reinstatement of Bahrain's National Assembly.

We would appreciate receiving information regarding the legal status of these eight individuals, and whether that status comports with Bahraini law.

We have been told of Bahraini citizens who allegedly have been dismissed from their jobs for signing public petitions advocating restoration of those provisions of Bahrain's constitution relating to the partially elected National Assembly. One such case is Professor Munira Fakhro, a sociologist who was dismissed from her position at Bahrain University in the fall of 1995. In the case Sa`id Asbool, an engineer and manager who was dismissed from his position in the Ministry of Public Works, we have been told that the authorities have also effectively prevented him from finding other employment in the public or private sectors.

We would appreciate any information the government can provide regarding the legal and employment status of these individuals and others who have allegedly been punished extrajudicially for exercising their right to freedom of expression. What rights of petition or redress do such individuals have?

(4) Access to legal counsel
HRW has spoken with many Bahrainis who have been detained by the authorities but who have been denied access to legal counsel while in detention and during interrogation. These individuals have told HRW, and Bahraini defense lawyers have confirmed, that persons charged and brought to trial in criminal and in security courts see a lawyer for the first time on the day of arraignment. We have been told that this is at minimum many months after they are initially detained, and that there are a number of instances when it has been as long as a year or more.

In cases that are remanded to the State Security Court, defendants in practice seem to have no access to legal counsel between court sessions. Bahraini lawyers have told us that there is no right of discovery in the security courts, and that lawyers and defendants are routinely denied adequate opportunity to prepare a defense.

We would appreciate any information you can provide regarding the law and practice concerning access by counsel to detainees. We would also appreciate your view as to whether present practice, particularly with regard to legal access for defendants before the security courts, meets Bahrain's obligations under international human rights law and under Bahrain's constitution.

(5) Treatment of detainees
HRW has spoken with a number of Bahrainis who have described a pattern of physical abuse in the process of arrest and while in detention. In several specific cases, detainees and lawyers have testified first-hand to extreme physical abuse amounting to torture. Concerns over physical abuse are heightened by the practice of incommunicado detention and reports of the acceptance of uncorroborated confessions as the basis for conviction in the security courts.

The recent agreement between the government and the International Committee of the Red Cross (ICRC) regarding ICRC access to Bahraini prisons seems to be a positive step. Has the government conducted any internal investigations into allegations of mistreatment during interrogation, particularly with regard to cases where detainees have died in detention, reportedly from torture and physical abuse? If so, could you inform us of the results of those investigations, and whether any responsible officials have been charged or disciplined in those cases?

(6) The State Security Law of 1974 and the State Security Court
Human Rights Watch is concerned that the court set up by Amiri Decree under Article 185 of the Penal Code, usually referred to as the State Security Court, and the implementation of the State Security Law of 1974, strips many of the safeguards against abuse. The law authorizes search, seizure and up to three years detention without charge or trial for a broadly defined range of offenses. The law further stipulates that "state security" proceedings "shall always be held *in camera*," and "without observing the procedures stipulated in the Law of Criminal Procedures." As we understand this law, access to legal counsel is nominal; no judicial review of the arrest and detention is permitted; the court may issue a conviction solely on the basis of uncorroborated confessions; and no appeals of the court's rulings are possible. Our concern is compounded by the fact that the public prosecutor, who decides whether a case should go to trial and whether it should go to the criminal or the security court, is attached directly to the Ministry of Interior.

We acknowledge that Bahrain's security concerns are real, and we agree that the government has the right to take measures to protect the safety of its citizens. We would nonetheless appreciate knowing the government's view of how the operation of the State Security Law of 1974 and the security courts can be reconciled with Bahrain's obligations under international human rights law and with Bahrain's constitution.

(7) Freedom of association
In early February 1996, according to news reports and accounts of Bahraini citizens, the government informed the Uruba Club, a preeminent Bahraini private association for the last sixty years, that it could not proceed with plans to conduct a seminar on the subject of "Shura and Democracy." A number of Bahraini citizens have told Human Rights Watch that the government closely controls meetings and gatherings, and that the government consistently rejects requests by authorized

organizations to hold meetings, whether public or closed to members of the club, to discuss current political issues. Similarly the government does not permit political parties or independent trade unions. Membership in or association with an unauthorized organization is an offense punishable under the State Security Law.

If your government compelled the Uruba Club to cancel its planned seminar on "Shura and Democracy" in February 1996, could you kindly share with us the basis for doing so? Would the government please comment on the allegation that no political organizations are allowed, and that authorized organizations, such as the Uruba Club, are not permitted to hold meetings or discussions dealing with Bahraini politics? To the extent that these claims are correct, how does this practice comport with Bahrain's obligations under international human rights law and Bahrain's constitution?

8) Monitoring human rights
The government has not responded positively to the standing request of Human Rights Watch, through Ambassador Ghaffar, to allow HRW to conduct a mission to Bahrain for the purpose of gathering information about the human rights situation in the country. We understand that the government has similarly rebuffed Amnesty International's request to visit the country. The request of the Bahrain Human Rights Organization, presently based in Copenhagen, to set up a public office in Bahrain has not, as far as we are aware, received a response.

Could you provide us with an explanation for the government's rejection to date of the request by Human Rights Watch to conduct an information-gathering visit? Will the government respond positively to requests by Bahraini citizens to monitor and report on human rights conditions in the country?

I believe that these questions fairly convey a sense of the scope of our forthcoming report, and some of its preliminary concerns. If you require any information from us prior to answering this letter, please do not hesitate to contact me at the above address. I thank you in advance for your attention to these matters, and hope to hear from you by April 1.

Yours sincerely,

Eric Goldstein
Acting Executive Director

Embassy
of the State of Bahrain
Washington
Office of the Ambassador

Ref. ....

                31st March, 1997
Date ....

الرقم ....

التاريخ ....

Mr. Eric Goldstein
Acting Executive Director
Human Rights Watch/Middle East
Human Rights Watch
1522 K Street, NW Suite 910
Washington, DC 20005

Dear Mr. Goldstein:

Thank you for your letter of 7th March, 1997. My Government appreciates
the opportunity to comment on allegations of human rights violations in
Bahrain prior to publication of your report on Bahrain.

We note with regret, that such an opportunity was denied prior to the
Human Rights Watch World Report 1997 - Events of 1996, published in
December, 1996. The Report was misinformed and was a long way from
presenting a true and balanced picture of the situation in Bahrain.

The Government of Bahrain shares the concerns of Human Rights Watch to
uphold and promote human rights internationally and fully respects Human
Rights Watch's efforts to identify the particular issues concerned.

The Government of the State of Bahrain is committed to protecting and
safeguarding the prosperity of all the citizens of Bahrain. It therefore views
your organization's reports with great interest and wishes to express its
concern that such reports should reflect the human rights situation in
Bahrain in an informed and balanced manner. My Government hopes

Human Rights Watch will cooperate with it and understand the real issues involved.

The reality is that Bahrain has recently witness a campaign of disturbance orchestrated by foreign backed terrorist groups. A serious conspiracy has been uncovered which revealed that the military wing of Hizbollah-Bahrain, together with Iranian backing, has been plotting and acting to undermine Bahrain's security and stability; its ultimate aim being to overthrow Bahrain's Government and replace it with a pro-Iranian regime. The conspiracy has not been limited to tangible acts of terrorism, but the roots go much deeper - to include sophisticated propaganda, information and financial networks.

The acts of terrorism carried out in Bahrain have caused the death of innocent people and the destruction of both private and public property. Since the conspiracy was unveiled in June, 1996, the country remains calm and united against the destabilization campaign it has been facing, and the situation in Bahrain is stable. The authorities will remain vigilant to counter any continuing threats, and I believe that Bahrain will continue to receive the widespread international support which it has enjoyed throughout for its resolute approach to addressing the problems which it has faced, and its determination to ensure peace and security in the country.

From the beginning of the destabilization campaign in late 1994, the activities of terrorists operating in Bahrain have been accompanied by allegations of human rights abuses on the part of the authorities in Bahrain. My Government, believing in the sanctity and preeminence of the United Nations, has strived to cooperate and promote dialogue with the United Nations Human Rights Commission, so as to clear its name of these unfounded allegations.

We have sought to explain the true situation in the region and to provide an understanding of the threat Bahrain has been facing. The allegations made against Bahrain originate from a very small, but skillful group of fundamentalist zealots and extremists, who are connected to terrorists in Bahrain. Some of these extremists are in self-imposed exile abroad. They have disseminated their propaganda through manipulation of the media and of the international human rights movement. The Government has always

2

maintained that these groups, while speaking of human rights, espouse a purely political agenda.

My Government hopes that - with this in mind - Human Rights Watch will understand the situation in Bahrain. In addressing your organization's concerns, my Government appeals, with respect and appreciation, for understanding.

1.   **Forced exile**

The alleged exile of political opponents is a non-issue. Bahrainis are not denied their rights of entry to or exit from Bahrain. A previous issue of disaffected Bahrainis involved in the 1981 pro-Iranian armed coup attempt in Bahrain was fully resolved by many of those returning under a Government plan during 1992-94. Those who did not return under that plan have either failed to establish their entitlement to Bahraini citizenship or have chosen otherwise. There is a strong core of violently pro-Iranian and anti-Bahraini revolutionaries active outside Bahrain. It is a fact that some of them returned to Bahrain under the Government plan with the sole purpose of organizing the recent terrorist / destabilization campaign. The issue is not political opposition. That again is a self pronounced description. The issue is maintenance of the integrity of the independent sovereign State of Bahrain and the right of the Bahraini people to live in peace in their own homeland.

2.   **Detention without trial or charges**

Allegations of mass arrests and arbitrary detention are unfounded and are recognized propaganda exercises. All arrests have been conducted by Bahrain's regular police force in the proper execution of their lawful duties to maintain law and order pursuant to article I of the Police Ordinance 1982 and in exercise of their lawful powers of arrest under Article XI of the Code of Criminal Procedure.

In every case the issues of detention, release, trial or imprisonment on conviction are determined by due process of the law including the automatic periodic judicial review of detention as required by law. My Government categorically assures Human Rights Watch that arbitrary detention is not practiced in Bahrain.

3.   **Freedom of Speech**

The Government has never categorized any offense as "political". The propagandist allegations of political causes have always proved to be violence related. The Government repeats that no-one has been arrested for their peaceful activities or beliefs (whether such beliefs are peaceful or not) and all those who have been arrested in connection with the troubles have been arrested for violence related activities contrary to specific articles of the 1976 Penal Code.

In your communication you mention Abdul Amir Al Jamri and seven others. Whilst I cannot comment on the facts of their individual cases as they are sub-judice, nevertheless I can confirm that all of the eight persons referred to are leading members of the terrorist group Hizbollah-Bahrain, primarily responsible for the terrorist campaign of violence and destruction. As for Ebrahim Adnan Nasir Al-Alawi, he is not in custody. They were not detained for expressing any political opinion or exercising their rights to freedom of speech, but for incitement of violence and other terrorist activities. Issues of their detention, trial and release are determined by due process of law. I can assure you that adequate legal, medical and procedural safeguard remain in full force and effect and that none of the men whom you name in your communication have been mistreated in any way. They are in good health, their conditions are humane and they are afforded all their right of visitation, welfare and medical care strictly in accordance with the law.

With regard to Munira Fakhro and Sa'id Asbool, I can assure you they were properly dismissed for abuses of their positions and acts incompatible with their professional responsibilities. Their dismissals were not for exercising their rights to freedom of expression.

4.   **Access to legal counsel**

All those arrested in connection with the recent unrest are dealt with by the due process of Bahrain's laws and either convicted by the independent courts or released. In the meantime, they are well treated, their conditions are humane and they are afforded all their rights of visitation and

4

representation strictly according to the law and are not held
incommunicado.

There is no question of denial of the rights of the accused to have access to
their lawyers at any time before or during proceedings, but it is a fact that
the role of defense lawyers in Bahrain inquisitorial jurisprudence is to
represent the accused during proceedings in court. Consequently, defense
lawyers are seldom engaged before the case is set down for trial and it is
rare for defense lawyers appointed early to seek interviews with their
clients.

How and when defense lawyers meet with their clients is of course entirely
a matter for them, but the courts will not try any case unless the defendants
are each represented by a defense lawyer willing to take their case
(appointed by the court if the defendant has none) and that each defending
lawyer has confirmed to the court that he is properly instructed by his client.

I wish to emphasize that defendants of whatever kind, whether involved in
State security offenses or normal criminal offenses, have the right to appoint
lawyers to represent them at any time after their arrest but in practice often
wait until they get to the trial court when the court is then bound by law to
appoint a defense lawyer for them free of charge.

5.   **Treatment of detainees**

Allegations that those arrested and detained by the Security Forces suffer
physical and mental abuse, or may be subjected to torture or other ill-
treatment, are simply not true, and propagandist in nature. My Government
has consistently addressed this long-standing theme over the recent period
of unrest.

The use of torture and undue force is, of course, unlawful and there are
internal procedures for the investigation of complaints against the police, in
addition to which, anyone so aggrieved has the right recourse to the courts
under the law. However, no-one has done so and no formal complaints
have been made.

I repeat that no-one is detained incommunicado. The State Security Court -
which is of course the High Court of Appeal and the highest judicial court

of trial - is bound by Article 5 of the Criminal Security Court Law of 1976 to weigh thoroughly any confession tendered in evidence. The court is also bound by the normal rules of evidence and must apply the 1966 Code of Criminal Procedure, which includes a provision that no confession made to a policeman shall be admitted in evidence. Accordingly, for a confession to be admissible to the court there must be corroboration.

Defense tactics need to be understood and considered when viewing allegations of coerced confessions. When faced with a defendant who has clearly made an admissible confession statement, the defense will routinely dispute the validity of that confession by alleging coercion and the courts concerned, including Remand courts, always order investigation of such allegations including medical examinations and reports. This inevitably leads to delays which is also part of the standard defense tactics in such situations.

6.   **State Security Law of 1974 and the State Security Court**

Allegations that Amiri Decree No.7 of 1976, establishing the Criminal Security Court, provides for unfair trials are an assertion by individuals and groups outside Bahrain, which act as fronts for terrorist groups.

The State Security Law of 1974 represents a formidable barrier to the terrorists and is therefore a constant target of terrorist propaganda. Without the security laws, the Government would not have the lawful basis upon which to effectively counter terrorism and acts of violence directed against the Bahraini community. Despite claims to the contrary, the State Security Law is not used either alone or in conjunction with any other law to deny any individual his right to a fair trial nor is it used to deny or prevent the peaceful exercise of any individual rights of freedom. There is, however, no legitimacy in the abuse of those rights by those who do so for violent purposes and those who do so in breach of the law will be dealt with in accordance with the law.

Such allegations have been thoroughly addressed by the Government in its November, 1992 Paper on the workings of the State Security Laws lodged with the United Nations Commission on Human Rights. This answers the concerns expressed in your communication.

7.   **Freedom of association**

Contrary to and despite the terrorist propaganda, the Government is dealing
with the situation in a fair and correct way compatible with the cultural and
ethical traditions and social and economic aspirations of the community,
including continued development towards constitutional or political
reforms. Your queries raise important issues but also reflect a lack of
understanding of the beliefs and practices of an Islamic society. My
Government would hope that greater understanding can be achieved through
meaningful dialogue but can assure you that we remain committed to the
principles enshrined in the Constitution of Bahrain. The laws of the land
reflect these principles and give full protection to the citizens' rights to
freedom of association. The Government is absolutely committed to the
development of the Consultative (Shura) Council and actively promotes
cooperation in the field of labor relations through comprehensive
legislation, the General Committee of Bahrain Workers and the Joint Labor-
Management Committees. Bahrain is also an active member of the
International Labor Organization.

8.   **Monitoring human rights**

My Government has no objection to visits in good faith by bona fide human
rights organizations arranged through the proper channels. We strongly
emphasize "good faith" and until there are effective demonstrations of good
faith then it is only natural that my Government will be wary of allowing
such visits. Requests by the Bahrain Human Rights Organization (BHRO)
to set an office in Bahrain are entirely false. No such request has ever been
made. The BHRO is not a bona fide Human Rights Organization and is run
by Abdul Hadi Abdullah Khawajha who is a trained terrorist and fugitive
from the 1981 failed armed coup living under asylum in Copenhagen. Full
details of these organizations and the individuals involved have been
provided to the United Nations Center for Human Rights.

The BHRO, the Committee for the Defense of Human Rights in Bahrain and
the Committee for the Defense of Political Prisoners in Bahrain are all one
and the same thing, merely being different names used as fronts by the
Denmark based propaganda wing of the Islamic Front for the Liberation of

7

Bahrain, formally also based in Damascus. They also act in concert with militant Hizbollah propagandists based in London.

The Government of Bahrain will use all means available within the law to protect its citizens. As a member of the United Nations, Bahrain fully recognizes its responsibilities to uphold fundamental human rights and freedoms in accordance with the United Nations Charter and the Universal Declaration of Human Rights.

I hope that this letter is of assistance in helping you to identify the real issues involved, and in alleviating your concerns. Should you require any further information or clarification, then I would be pleased to assist. I wish to stress that the door for dialogue is open and I hope Human Rights Watch will seize the opportunity to foster a relationship of cooperation and understanding with my Government.

Yours sincerely,

DR. MUHAMMAD ABDUL GHAFFAR
Ambassador of the State of Bahrain